Kama Sutra Woman

Kama

Sutra Woman

Eleanor McKenzie

hamlyn

First published in Great Britain in 2006 by

Hamlyn, a division of Octopus Publishing Group Ltd

2–4 Heron Quays, London E14 4JP

Copyright © Octopus Publishing Group Ltd 2006

ISBN-13: 978-0-600-61402-9

ISBN-10: 0-600-61402-6

A CIP catalogue record for this book is available from the British Library

Printed and bound in China

10 9 8 7 6 5 4 3 2 1

Contents

Introduction

Pleasures are as necessary for the wellbeing of the body as food.

Welcome to the *Kama Sutra* for women. So you've picked up this book, perhaps intrigued by the title, but how much do you really know about *Kama Sutra*? Around two thousand years ago, the sage Mallinaga Vatsyayana wrote what was to become the best known text ever devoted to sensual pleasure or 'The Science of Love': 'Kama' because this conveyed enjoying the world using the mind and soul as well as all five senses; 'Sutra' because this meant life-enhancing spiritual teachings.

So how relevant is this ancient wisdom to us? Orientalist and erotica enthusiast Sir Richard Burton, who also translated *The Perfumed Garden*, was the first to translate and publish the *Kama Sutra* in the West in 1883. Although he shared his interest in erotica with like-minded Victorian gentlemen, part of its appeal was that it was a guilty pleasure. The West still had some way to go before it could deal with sex as openly as the ancient Hindus had. In fact, we were not ready for the *Kama Sutra* until the 1960s.

What's in it for us?

Why *Kama Sutra* for women? Vatsyayana wrote the *Kama Sutra* during a time of male dominance. Although he encourages women to study it and become proficient in the art of love, much of it is written from the male perspective, teaching the woman how to kiss, give oral sex and achieve positions. Although this in itself is erotic, most of the text is not concerned with the woman's pleasure. Still, the approach chimes in with female sexuality, because it recognizes that there is more to sex than the basic bump 'n' grind.

The many sexual positions for which it is famous form only a small part of the *Kama Sutra*. The complete text is far broader: it is a guide to mastering the senses and to healthy sexual conduct within society. However, for our purposes the section of the text called The Embrace is most relevant. It covers all the basic aspects of sensual pleasure in some detail as well as including weird and wonderful variations such as scratching, biting and striking the body.

In the Victorian era the *Kama Sutra* was still being used to satisfy men's lusts, but Vatsyayana's joyful celebration of sex is sensual enough to be read from a female perspective, too.

In this edition, we concentrate on what brings women the most pleasure. It's time for women to find out what's in it for them.

'...it's time for women to find out what's in it for them.'

What today's woman wants

Today we want satisfaction. We also want to be able to explore and express our sexuality with confidence. But we need help. We all begin with misinformation about sex: the great 'truths' that circulated around the schoolyard. Then, once we start having sex, we think we know all we need to. But our sexuality is an expression of our self, and we never stop learning about that.

Making the most of the *Kama Sutra*

The *Kama Sutra* is a guide. This book takes the bare bones of its teachings and adapts them for today's woman, helping us to give and receive more intense pleasure than ever before. Focusing on that essential female element, like the original *Kama Sutra* this book recognizes the importance of the art of seduction – not only the basics like getting the mood right with music and aroma, but also ensuring that the food is tasty and the conversation stimulating.

The sexual positions have all been described with women's pleasure in mind. Subtle movements and changes in position can make all the difference. Much as the book follows the spirit of the *Kama Sutra*, it should be regarded as an attitude of mind and a set of options rather than something that must be followed to the letter. Some postures are difficult. Feel free to experiment and adapt, just as you might when you are following a recipe and find you are missing an ingredient. It's all about expression.

So who is a *Kama Sutra* woman?

A *Kama Sutra* woman studies courtship and love with the dedication of an artist, forever mixing the colours on her palette to make new ones. She prides herself on her creativity and her ability to give pleasure while learning how to surrender herself to receiving it. She follows this teaching of the *Kama Sutra*:

Variety is necessary in love, so love is to be produced by means of variety. It is on this account that courtesans who are well acquainted with the various ways and means become so desirable, for if variety is sought in all the arts and amusements, how much more so should it be sought after in love.

Women need good, honest information about sex and its possibilities. They have the right to know that sexual taste is diverse and that sexual appetite has no conception of 'normal'. It is neither about pleasing men nor pleasing yourself; it's a shared experience. Learning to let go and explore your boundaries takes a little courage and lots of practise.

Dip your toe into some alternative ideas. Have fun.

'...this book takes the bare bones of the **Kama Sutra** teachings and adapts them for today's woman.'

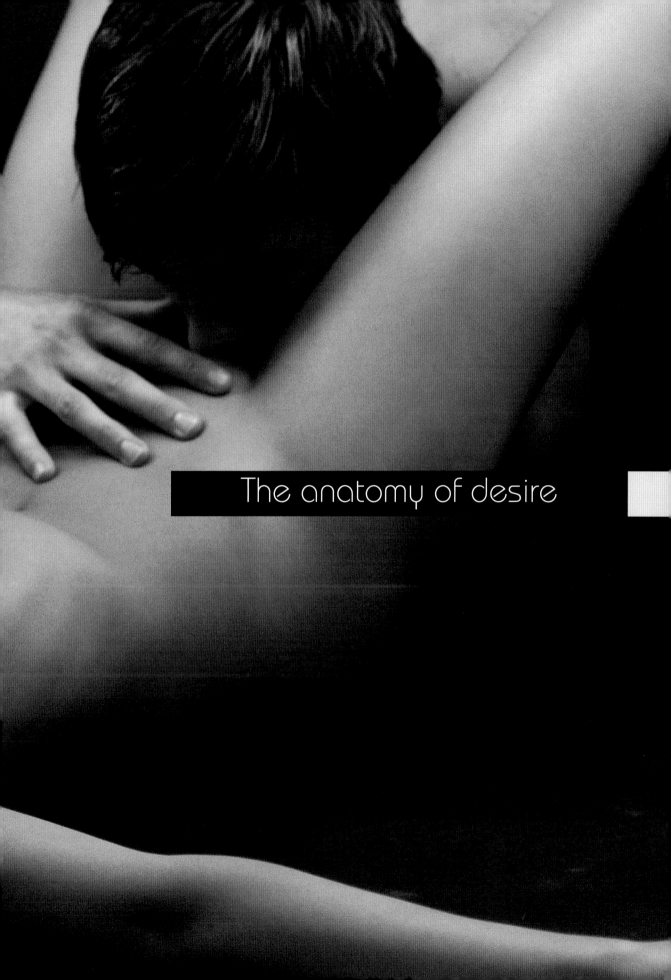

The anatomy of desire

The art of attraction

He only is her true husband who possesses the qualities that are liked by her...because he is the husband of love.

We all know that mysterious 'oomph' feeling when we are attracted to someone, but how do we attract a person to us, and to what extent do we have any control over it? The attraction appears random but the reason that one stranger appeals to us more than another partly relates to our ideas about ourselves. Our appreciation of the way a man is dressed is a reflection of our own style and how we perceive it. If a man is dressed very differently we are less likely to be attracted to him, and vice versa.

If you look closely at a couple's faces, you will often see uncanny similarities. Looks, posture and your man's general vibe will usually reflect something of yourself, and other people that you have been close to in the past and feel comfortable with.

Women have always struggled with the question of how to attract men and stay attractive to them. Centuries of conditioning have told us that our physical appearance is central to our attractiveness, and that our survival in the world is dependent on it. This has made us emotionally vulnerable: if we were not, the cosmetics industry would not wield the power that it does.

It is beneficial to look good and make the most of your appearance, but only because this reflects how you feel about yourself. At the same time, each woman must be confident that it is all of her which is attractive, and that it is this confidence that attracts men. Women who are happy with themselves attract more men, and men who are right for them. What is more, a man knows that a confident, happy woman is a good lover.

Sex styles

There are two aspects of this. First, there are general sex styles – put crudely, fast sex, soft sex and energetic sex. Second, there is the individual's personal style.

Generally we should aim for variety. Patterns that emerge tend to be established in the first few months of the relationship. These can be hard to break, resulting in routine that takes all the excitement out of sex. Take a good, honest look at the pattern of your sex life and – gently! – tell your partner about any changes you'd like to make to it. Ask them how they feel about it.

Your personal sex style may also have been established early on and needs a revamp from time to time. There are always new techniques to be acquired and things to be tried. Developing your sex style is like working on toning your body: it needs to be done regularly. One last thing: if you and a new lover have incompatible sex styles and neither of you is able to adapt, compromise or even discuss it, this does not augur well for a long-term relationship. The modern woman wants satisfaction – not frustration.

'...women who are happy with themselves attract more men, and men who are right for them.'

The woman aroused

It can be difficult for a man to spot when a woman is aroused. She does not have a loud, proud erection on display for all to see. This is why the *Kama Sutra* begins to describe the signs of arousal in women. It says:

Her body relaxes, she closes her eyes, she puts aside all bashfulness and shows increased willingness to unite the two organs as closely as possible.

But that's not all. Her pupils dilate, her breathing speeds up and her temperature rises. She may even get a deep red flush before there is any sexual contact. And these are just the visible signs. Her clitoris may be tingling and her vaginal juices may be starting to build up in preparation for penetration.

There are other visual cues a man can look out for. If you are talking to someone who is making you feel aroused, you are likely to touch yourself around the breasts and genitals, or draw attention to them in some other way. Similarly, when you want to be kissed, you will touch or wet your lips. Playing with your hair is another sign that you want to be touched. Some men are very attuned to this body talk; others are oblivious.

Clearly, what you do with your arousal depends on the situation: you can initiate sex or keep it on a slow burn, building it up until you have to act.

In touch with your body
Since most women have love/hate relationships with their bodies and tend to be critical of certain parts of them, they can be reluctant to get in touch with them. It's surprising how few women actually look at their genitals. Yet have you ever noticed how often a man looks at his genitals and touches them, even in public? They love theirs, and we need to learn to love ours too, if we are ever to feel comfortable with ourselves.

In the age of the digital camera we can photograph our genitals and look at them in different states of arousal. Before and after climax pictures will show you the changes and help you to see the beauty of your vulva. Men are able to appreciate it and adore being able to look at it. Being relaxed about your partner admiring it will make you a more confident lover. Indulge your curiosity. Look at pictures of other women's vulvas if you can and become aware of the many variations that exist.

Women tend to touch their bodies when they masturbate, but this is localized touching with a specific aim in mind. It does not get you in touch with how your whole body feels. How often do we stroke our arms, legs or breasts and admire them, or experiment with how different types of touch create different responses?

One way to get in touch with your body is to spend time getting to know it when you are naked. The best way to learn to appreciate it this way, and thereby increase your ease with it, is by sitting in front of a mirror while you explore and admire.

'...her body relaxes, she closes her eyes, she puts aside all bashfulness and shows increased willingness to unite the two organs as closely as possible.'

Special scents

Our sense of smell is highly developed and the fastest of our five senses. We secrete pheromones that identify us as human and each living creature has its own scent, helping them to locate each other. Our sense of smell is dull compared with that of other animals – a dog can locate a human beneath mounds of rubble just by using its nose.

Men are highly aroused by the scent of a woman: her natural scent combined with that of her sexual juices can be a real turn-on. Here is a useful tip for turning him on while you're out on a date: dab on your usual perfume and then put your finger inside your vagina, cover it in your natural secretions and then dab this over the same places as your perfume, paying particular attention to the pulse points on the neck, as he will pick the scent up best from this area. He will be unaware that you have done this, and he will be wondering why he can't wait to get you somewhere private. This is a particularly good trick to use if he seems disinterested in sex.

Other scents that are a turn-on for both of you may be a matter of individual taste. However, there are some that never seem to fail – vanilla is one of these. Go carefully, because it can be quite sweet and overpowering. One way to incorporate it into sex play is to put a vanilla pod in a glass of champagne, or make up a massage oil with vanilla aromatherapy oil in it. Sandalwood is described by the *Kama Sutra* as the perfect scent to massage your lover's body with before sex, although it is interesting that in a culture known for its use of scented ointments it does not recommend any others.

Good aromatherapy oils are widely available and can be used to create a seductive ambience in a room. The oils considered most aphrodisiac are jasmine, clary sage, frankincense, geranium, lavender, patchouli, sandalwood, ylang ylang and, lastly, the goddess of all oils – rose otto. This is a very precious and expensive oil, but its effect on a man's libido makes it worth every penny. You can either use a burner to scent a room, or you could make your own spray with warm water and oil.

Unless you know what you are doing, be mindful of combining too many essential oils at once – you might create a completely different effect to the desired one. Most aphrodisiac oils are quite intense, which means they can also give some people a headache.

Modern perfumes are based on many of these aphrodisiac oils and those considered particularly sexy often have patchouli, sandalwood or ylang ylang notes in them. Many women now have a wardrobe of scents that they wear for different occasions, preferring the lighter, cleaner flower or fruit fragrances such as lily or grapefruit for the day and a much heavier, headier scent for the evening.

However, there is nothing like the scent of a clean, warm body after a bath or shower: this is a very powerful turn-on for most people.

'...men are highly aroused by the scent of a woman: her natural scent combined with that of her sexual juices can be a real turn-on.'

Mirrors

The smooth surface of water and polished metal were the earliest mirrors. The *Kama Sutra* may not be aware of the sexual potency of the mirror, yet we can imagine that the still pond in the courtyard of a Sultan's palace, and the highly polished silver and gemstones sewn onto the sari of a harem girl, all evoked the eroticism of reflection and being looked at.

Traditionally women are supposed to love standing in front of mirrors admiring themselves, but not so when they are naked. The changing room syndrome illustrates this perfectly: who has not had a moment of horror on catching sight of parts of herself that are rarely seen. However, we can learn to make a full-length mirror our friend.

You will need to find some time alone when you know you will not be disturbed. Create a special ambience by scenting the room and making it warm and comfortable. Candlelight is gentler than electric light and will help ease you into the process of getting to know your body.

Undress, and shower or bathe to make yourself aware of your body. Afterwards, wrap yourself in a warm, fluffy towel or bathrobe. You might want to use body lotion or oil to help you in your exploration. Make yourself comfortable in front of the mirror, and begin by touching and stroking the visible parts of your body one by one. As you stroke each part, really look at it;

notice where the skin changes colour and where there are small marks or lines. As you stroke, become aware of the texture of your skin and where it changes. If you are becoming aroused, note what is doing it for you.

Now remove your towel and start with your breasts. Examine them, cup them and feel the weight of them; play with your nipples by pulling and rubbing them. Become familiar with the curves of your breasts, and raise and lower your arms to see how they change shape. Run your hands down over your ribcage and belly, feeling the softness of it. Pay attention to your thighs, inside and out, your lower legs, ending with your feet, which do so much hard work for you and at the same time are among the most erotic, sensitive parts of your body.

Finally, turn to your genitals. You may need to use a small hand mirror to examine them. Some lubricant may help you. At first, just look at the petal-like forms of the labia covering your opening. Now use your fingers to study your clitoris, and pull the labia apart gently to reveal the vagina. Insert your fingers and see how this looks. Feel the texture and heat of the inside of your vagina. This warmth and moisture is what your lover likes to feel enfold him snugly.

You can finish by sitting still and admiring your body, its uniqueness and its natural lines – or you can make yourself come.

'...stand in front of a mirror and admire your body, its uniqueness and its natural lines.'

Masturbation

The women of the royal harem...accomplish their object by means of bulbs, roots and fruits having the form of the lingam, or they lie down upon the statue of a male figure on which the lingam is visible and erect.

It is important that women give themselves pleasure by bringing themselves to climax. Not only does it teach us about what pleases us, which we in turn can teach our lovers, but it is also very good for our health. An orgasm a day circulates energy around the body, increases the heart rate and relieves stress and tension in the body. What a lovely way to stay healthy.

Vary your techniques as this will increase your sensitivity and response to your lover when he touches you. Some women are fearful that constant use of a vibrator will make them unresponsive to their lover. However, experts are agreed that these fears are unfounded. Alternating between using a vibrator and your fingers will ensure that you keep in touch with your clitoris's responses.

Becoming aware of the amount of pressure you like is important. For example, some women like very light pressure to begin with changing to stronger, more constant pressure as she feels herself about to come. Men are often unaware of this need for constant pressure as a woman is about to orgasm and need to be told about it, as it is easy for a woman to lose her climax if the pressure is taken off.

The pressure of water from the shower directed on the clitoris is another interesting way to masturbate and creates a different range of sensations from manual stimulation. Similarly, try out different positions for masturbation. Everyone has ones that work for them and ones that don't – lying on your back with your legs apart isn't the only way. Try sitting on a chair with your legs tightly together and stroke yourself through your clothing. You can come like this, especially if you are already feeling aroused. You could also try a technique of 'drumming' either side of the clitoris with your index and middle finger; this produces an orgasm quickly.

If you have problems with masturbation and find it difficult to climax, or want to increase your chances of multiple orgasm, here is an Eastern technique to help you to loosen up and become more aroused. It is a simple system of breathing based on the idea that when you are exhaling, you are breathing out fear, and when you inhale you focus on all the pleasurable sensations in your body and send the breath to them. As you feel yourself approaching orgasm, use your breath to take you into it, breathing past any emotional blocks that are holding you back. It is essential for women who want to achieve orgasm with ease to learn how to move out of their heads and into their bodies.

Once you feel comfortable with this technique you might like to try it with your lover. Ask him to stimulate you while you concentrate on your breathing and the way your body feels. Focusing on breathing helps the mind to stop chattering and allows you to be more aware of your body and its surroundings. Our minds have a way of cutting us off from many experiences, from hearing the birds singing to sexual pleasure.

Lastly, mutual masturbation or taking turns to watch each other is highly erotic. Consciously allowing your lover to watch you climax, and to see your facial expression fully as you come is a wonderful way of deepening the intimacy between you.

'...it is important that women give themselves pleasure by bringing themselves to climax.'

Fantasy

While the *Kama Sutra* doesn't cover the role of fantasy in sex, in the past few decades we have begun to recognize its importance. There had always been a tendency to think that only men indulged in sexual fantasies, but the emergence of erotic novels for women and books on women's fantasies has put paid to that idea.

When it comes to sexual fantasies, men and women are decidedly different in their tastes. Men's fantasies tend to involve strangers rather than women they know, group sex and almost always get down to penetration pretty quickly.

By contrast, women's tend to include extended foreplay and their regular partner, and the focus is on the emotional relationship between the people in the fantasy. In this respect, women's fantasies tend to reflect their real-life behaviour rather more than men's do.

Fantasy provides us with a very healthy form of release and is an excellent way to explore your sexuality – as long as you are not fearful. Within the privacy of your own mind it is perfectly safe to imagine what you will, and in the process have great sex.

Sharing your fantasies with a partner is clearly an intimate thing to do and only you can judge when the time is right to do so. Go gently, and be sure not to introduce anything that might make your partner feel threatened. But when it feels appropriate, sharing what turns you on in your imagination reveals more of you to him and helps him to pleasure you more. Exchanging fantasies in a frank way also strengthens your bond.

Deciding to act out a favourite fantasy with a partner can be sexually intoxicating. As with dressing up (see pages 62–71) you can reveal aspects of yourself that are normally hidden. Fantasy role-play is particularly exciting when done in a public place. You might meet up in a hotel bar having adopted different personas: you change your name, your background, your job and perhaps dress in a different way.

You can then approach each other and start the seduction process from scratch. You will probably find that this permits you to talk sexually in a way that you wouldn't otherwise and that the sexual tension builds between you both very quickly. You might decide to check in to the hotel – sex in a different location heightens the experience. But role-playing can just as easily be done at home. It depends on your taste and circumstances.

Fantasy role-play has only one rule: sex is the natural end to your play – after that, drop your identities. When a lover is willing to share a fantasy with you and act it out, it is a privilege that must be respected. There is a delicate magic in role-play that needs to be preserved so that you can use the memories of it to arouse each other in the future.

'...fantasy provides us with a very healthy form of release and is an excellent way to explore your sexuality.'

The clitoris

The clitoris is not a modern invention, it clearly existed at the time of the *Kama Sutra*. However, it is only in recent years that its importance has been understood, hence the silence about it in ancient texts. Freud didn't do much to help things either with his insistence on the supremacy of the vaginal orgasm. Thanks to him it was assumed that orgasm originated in the vagina, and the myth of the superior vaginal orgasm persists today, despite widespread information about the clitoris.

The clitoris is your centre of pleasure. Like the penis, it consists of erectile tissue made up of blood vessels, spongy tissue and nerve endings. Also like the penis, it enlarges and becomes erect when stimulated. It is the only organ of the human body whose sole function is the experience of sexual pleasure.

It is very sensitive. Fortunately it is also well protected by its hood and the fleshy mons veneris (the area covered by pubic hair). Over-stimulation of the clitoris is painful for most women, which is why we must teach men how to touch it. Men tend to like a firm grip when you are stimulating their penis and some men treat the clitoris like it was a penis. Hard rubbing makes the clitoris retreat, and nobody wants that.

Encourage your lover to use some form of lubricant on your clitoris before stimulating it manually, as this will feel more comfortable and you will be able to relax and enjoy the pleasure you are receiving. Men often use their saliva to lubricate women, but this dries up quickly, so keep some almond oil close to hand.

Most women cannot come without the clitoris being stimulated. This does not mean that it always has to be touched directly though. In fact, around and across the clitoris is often more pleasurable. However, some forms of indirect stimulation, such as the thrust of your lover against your pubic mound while, say, in the Missionary position, does not generally touch the clitoris enough to make you climax. This is why

positions in which one of you can touch the clitoris or the area around it are preferable if you want to achieve orgasm during penetration. Every woman's anatomy and response to stimulation is unique, so you will need to experiment with positions to find out what works for you.

Finally, if you don't climax during penetration, ask your lover to help you get there after he has come. Feeling frustrated and angry is no way to end sex.

The G-spot

The G-spot was 'discovered' around 1982 and made its way into popular sex mythology as some kind of button that when pressed resulted in mind-blowing ecstasy. Consequently, everyone started looking for it.

The location of the G-spot is on the front wall of the vagina. If you hook your middle finger inside you will find a small, spongy mass which has a different texture to the rest of your vagina. This is it. Rub it and you will probably feel like having a pee. This is because it is really a piece of sponge wrapped around the urethra.

Some women love having it stimulated and find that it heightens their pleasure, while others find it irritating, probably because it makes them want to go to the bathroom. G-spot stimulation can make women ejaculate. This happens when a lover has taken a lot of time to stimulate both the clitoris and G-spot orally and manually. For many women, the sensation of ejaculating while climaxing is exquisite – once they have got over the fear that they have wet themselves.

Try stimulating your G-spot yourself using your fingers or a vibrator – it can produce a very intense orgasm. Sex positions that are good for G-spot pleasure are rear entry ones, but if you are lying on your back, you might find that placing your legs between your partner's rather than outside them will also provide you with some very pleasant G-spot sensations.

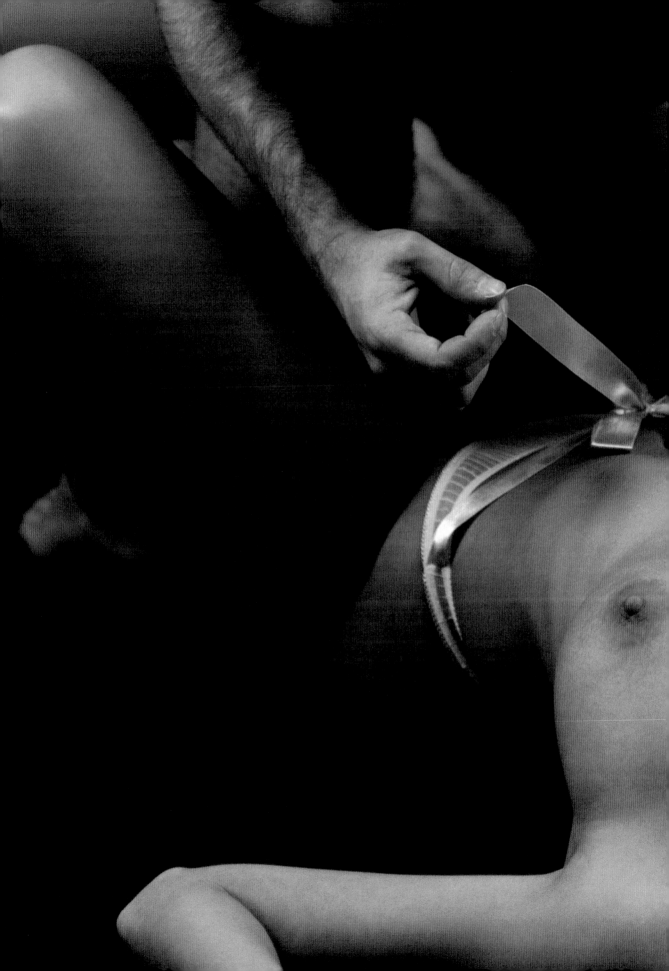

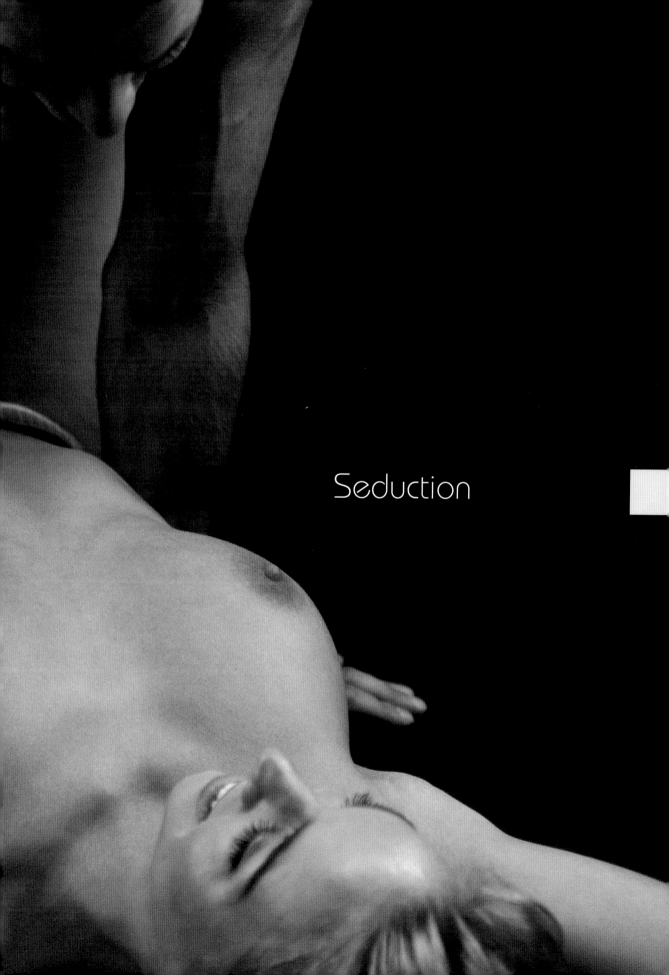

Seduction

Love or lust?

It's one of those $64 million questions: Is what you're experiencing love or lust? How can you tell the difference, and are men more frequently 'in lust' than 'in love'?

In the *Kama Sutra* it is assumed that men have stronger sexual urges and that marriage and the sexual practices described in the text will keep a man from following his lusts. This in turn will result in him having a steady life and being well respected by society. Some women are categorized in the *Kama Sutra* as being full of lust and these women are to be avoided, it says – marrying them will cause you trouble.

Lust can hit either sex at any time, but learn how to spot this before you fall in love. So, how can you tell the difference? If you are fixated on having sex with him every time you see him but find him uninteresting in other ways then you are most likely in lust. If sex is the only thing cementing your relationship then you need to be honest with yourself and admit that this is a purely physical attraction, unlikely to develop into anything more meaningful. There's nothing wrong with having a lust relationship as long as you recognize it as such. Sometimes it's good to indulge in the release of the purely physical without emotional attachment.

Love is more difficult to identify. Artists, poets and musicians have all tried to help us define it over the centuries, yet still its definition is elusive. Love is...what you believe it to be. In the *Kama Sutra* it is written that there are ten symptoms of being in love that increase in their intensity as the passion progresses. The symptoms start with attraction of the eye and progress to starvation and finally death if the love is not requited.

Sex is an important element of a loving relationship, yet in the early stages of a relationship it can make us confused about whether we love someone or not. If the sex is good we have a tendency to think we will work in the long term as a couple. But it could just be lust. We may use sex to fulfill our emotional needs and convince ourselves that this is love. But we are fooling ourselves if we rely on this as a guide.

Love arises more from friendship, from being able to spend time with a person and from wanting to be with them even when they do something annoying. When we love someone, we are able to see beyond their imperfections. As Shakespeare wrote, 'Love is not love which alters when it alteration finds.' (Sonnet 116.) In other words, a relationship may have its ups and downs, but if it is based on love it will survive.

Supporting each other's dreams and visions through the good and bad times is a mark of love. A partner who believes in what you want to achieve with your life is one to cherish because this indicates the lack of selfishness which is necessary for love to survive in the long term. And, if you have the same belief in them then you will probably know you are in love.

Still, some lust is required to get a relationship going and the hormones involved in creating that unique sensation of lusting after someone are working overtime to bring men and women together. If these hormones were not at work we may never be attracted to men. So, lust gets us going, but it does not keep us going.

'...love is not love which alters when it alteration finds.'
Sonnet 116, William Shakespeare (1564–1616)

Getting to know each other

The *Kama Sutra* does not go into detail about the beginnings of a relationship. This reflects the fact that marriages were arranged and the couple would only get to know each other after they had been married. So it concentrates more on how the man may introduce his wife to sex.

For example, in the section on how to begin or end sex, it suggests:

In the pleasure room...the man should receive the woman...and invite her to take refreshment and to drink freely...they should then carry on an amusing conversation...and may also talk suggestively. They may sing...talk about the arts. At last, when the woman is overcome with desire...they should proceed to congress.

This train of events takes place in the course of an evening, but it can also be applied to dating that takes place over several weeks, or until you feel a relationship has been established. Trouble sometimes occurs when people's opinions of when this is vary: some feel they are in a relationship after the second meeting, while others take months to feel a relationship has been established.

Today everything happens so quickly. Yet in relationships slow is almost always best. Taking time to get to know a man before you become too emotionally involved can save you a lot of pain later. Yes, there are times when people meet and just fall in love, but instantaneous love that stands the test of time is rare.

What does getting to know a person involve? For a start, is he your best friend? Do you have much in common? And, very importantly, does your vision of your future blend with his?

You can only tell if he is going to be your best friend over time. You will have your own values regarding friendship: does he fulfill them? Also, how much do you really have in common? Sharing a love for a particular CD may not be enough to cement a relationship in the long term but at the beginning it's a sign that your tastes are similar. Nobody will share your values, tastes and dreams one hundred per cent, so it is important to discover if you can both compromise over and tolerate those things you don't have in common.

Lastly, having a common goal for the future is good for a long-term relationship. Get to know what he wants and see how well it fits in with your plans before you commit yourself to a serious relationship. If you suddenly find you want different things out of life, you could find your futures taking very different paths.

'...taking time to get to know a man before you become too emotionally involved can save you a lot of pain later.'

Courtship

Not so long ago, courtship was still a well-defined sequence of events. Everyone knew the rules and what was required of them and when. The sexual revolution, particularly the availability of contraception for women, changed all that. So, does courtship have any meaning for the modern woman, and what might contemporary courtship entail?

One interpretation of the advice from the *Kama Sutra* is that entertainment of your lover, and communication with him, are the most significant elements of courtship. Entertainment can take any number of forms, the most obvious one being culinary. Cook for him. If he wants to cook for you early on in your relationship, the chances are you are being seduced. If he pays attention to your likes and dislikes, he's a keeper.

The *Kama Sutra* suggests you entertain your lover by reading poetry and playing musical instruments. That's all well and good, but if he isn't into poetry, you have no musical talent and a band that you both like is not playing in town, a good substitute is giving him a massage. Massage can be part of sex, but it doesn't have to be, and a head or foot massage can be given while he's watching TV. Let him know how you like things done – get him to give you a foot massage, feed you chocolates and pour you wine. It's not rocket science – purr appreciatively when he does, and he'll do it again.

Make each other feel like you're the only two people in the world. Everybody loves being made to feel special, and you deserve it!

Attention to detail works wonders in courtship. Everyone is familiar with the mind-blowing impact of someone remembering something you noticed in a shop and buying it for your birthday, or buying you the particular newspaper you read on that particular day. Observe what he drinks, and fix his drink that way. Observe his routines and slot yourself in with them as far as you can – as long as it's a two-way street. You will have your own quirks, and if the relationship is to have a happy future, he will be observing these in the same way.

Written communication used to be a very important aspect of courtship, and lovers would exchange love notes regularly. These would typically be kept so that they could be read repeatedly. To receive a handwritten note, however brief, is still a delight, even more so now, when so few people write. Similarly, leaving little notes for your lover in unexpected places will please him, particularly if you are going to be away for a time. But now, in place of scented paper, we have courtship by email and text message. Both are extremely valuable modes of communication. As is the quick phone call just to say 'I miss you.'

So thoughtfulness and attention are the two qualities everyone should bring to courtship.

'...does courtship have any meaning for the modern woman, and what might contemporary courtship entail?'

Women take the lead

For as long as most people can remember it has been assumed that men should take the lead in establishing a relationship, and that it would be somehow unfeminine for a woman to adopt the same role. With the modern day woman having been liberated from very traditional roles, she is now expected to do as men do in many respects. However, because of this, there is a very real sense in which women are struggling to define being a woman, especially in relationship to men.

Naturally, the *Kama Sutra* reflects the old order of things: the man in a supreme position. It says of the virtuous wife:

A virtuous woman...should act in conformity with his wishes as if he were a divine being. She should keep the whole house well cleaned and arrange flowers in different parts of it, and make the floor smooth and polished so as to give the whole a neat and becoming appearance. The wife...should lead a chaste life, devoted to her husband and doing everything for his welfare.

Not exactly a vision of women's liberation.

But if both parties heed the advice then you're in a good relationship. We are all divine beings. Ancient and modern writers on relationships agree that you will greatly improve your relationship with your lover if you are mindful of the fact that he is, in a way, a living god. Just as you are the living manifestation of the goddess.

In the Namaste posture on pages 122–123, the man honours the woman as divine, while in Maharajah (see pages 114–115) she treats him as king. Showing your devotion to your lover does not mean you have sold out to the 'surrendered wife' movement, which advises women to completely obey their husbands in all things. There is true surrender and there is the pretence of it, which is really a form of subjection.

Visualizing yourself as a living goddess is one way to approach taking the lead role. This does not mean identifying solely with being the 'leader', but rather taking your rightful turn in sustaining the relationship and not leaving it all up to the man. Knowing when you need to take over and doing so gracefully is an art form for the modern woman to master in her relationships.

There are plenty of goddesses to choose from if you need inspiration. You might choose to identify with Radha, the lover of Krishna, who is often portrayed in the woman-on-top position. Their relationship is described as a passionate struggle with Krishna who, over time, found ways to satisfy the fiery Radha and remove her jealousy. Then there is the devoted Sita, the wife of Rama, who demonstrated her absolute fidelity to him by walking through fire. There is also Padma, the Venus of India whose voluptuous body was revered as that of the ideal woman. There are also the goddesses of the Greek myths: sexy Aphrodite and independent-minded and athletic Artemis to name the two most appropriate for modern women. And if the goddesses of religion and mythology don't appeal to you, try the more contemporary sex goddesses such as Marilyn Monroe, Madonna or the sultry Sophia Loren. Those that capture your imagination will reveal quite a lot to you about your sexuality and how you wish to reveal it to your partner.

'...knowing when you need to take over and doing so gracefully is an art form for the modern woman to master in her relationships.'

Communicating with your senses

Sight

The *Kama Sutra* says the first symptom of love is 'attraction of the eye'. Whether it turns out to be love or not, attraction certainly starts with our visual sense. Most impressions are formed within the first few minutes, even seconds, of seeing someone. We then combine these impressions with information we have stored in our memories and make a decision about them.

What are we looking at that can draw us so powerfully to another person? It is a number of things: we may be attracted to them in a primal way for their facial symmetry or strength, which suggest good genes; their posture may do it for us; or their dress sense. All of these are analyzed by us to see if they fit with our idea of what we are looking for in a partner. We would be amazed at all the elements that form our conclusion.

It's a well-known fact that we are attracted to people who have a comparable level of attractiveness to our own. We can also often tell by looking if they come from a similar social background to our own or are likely to have a similar value system. They may resemble one of our parents in some way. This becomes more apparent as you get to know them, but nevertheless, you may have recognized it at some level the first time you look at them. Basically, we are attracted to people who are familiar.

Indian women at the time of the *Kama Sutra* would loosen their hair and reveal a little more cleavage once they were aware they had a man's attention. So, revealing more of yourself as you become aware of his gaze is not exactly a new thing. You might want to follow their lead by subtly revealing parts of your body as time goes on and experimenting with translucent clothes and sensual fabrics. Remember, less is more – a little bit of cleavage, a glimpse of thigh. Don't be too obvious.

Catching someone's eye is the first step in communicating with them. When you hold their gaze for just a fraction longer than usual, you have signalled your interest. Your pupils will dilate, and if they return your gaze without looking away, you know you can proceed with your next sense.

Hearing

We often use sound as an expression of desire. The *Kama Sutra* says of the aroused woman:

During the excitement she continually utters words expressive of...desire of liberation...intermingled with the sighing, weeping and thundering sounds.

We know the sounds that people make during sex, but what information do we pick up about a partner in other situations?

The first time you hear his voice you will take in further information about him. His accent is not as important as the quality of his voice. If the pitch of his voice is light we may judge it slightly feminine, from the outset this is a bad sign. It won't get any better.

Hearing is also listening to your lover and learning his communication style. We know men and women have very different styles of communication and that it is remarkably easy for us to misunderstand each other. Making time to talk is also very important. Things left undiscussed have a way of erupting at moments when they are likely to cause friction, when they could have been discussed calmly at a time when your partner was receptive. Knowing when it is a good time to talk is a skill based on experience of your partner.

'...catching someone's eye is the first step in communicating with them.'

Touch

Touch, in the *Kama Sutra*, is part of the work of a man giving pleasure to a woman. It says:

...he should loosen the knots of her under garments, and when she begins to dispute him, he should overwhelm her with kisses. Then when he is erect he should touch her with his hands in various places and gently manipulate various parts of the body.

Touch is a very powerful form of communication. The lightest touch on the arm or hand signals that your lover really wants you to listen to him, and you know your attention is important to him. This type of simple touch is a way of increasing the intimacy between you.

Touch signals caring. We only touch, and want to be touched by, those people we are happy to bring very close to us. We are all familiar with the feeling of unease that arises when somebody we don't like touches us.

Touch is also healing. Your lover's embrace can remove all the stresses you are holding in your body and give you the comfort and emotional warmth we all need so much. Wanting to be hugged and cuddled doesn't make a person needy, neither is it necessarily sexual. You should be able to use your sense of touch with your lover without it meaning that you want sex. Some people hold back from touching simply because they fear that any touch will be construed as being sexual. This is one of the reasons we are all suffering from a hunger to experience the comfort of another's touch.

Smell

At the beginning of sexual union, according to the *Kama Sutra*, 'the man should apply with his own hand to the body of a woman some pure sandalwood ointment'. Sandalwood is known to have aphrodisiac qualities and for many people it is an extremely evocative scent. Similarly, we know from descriptions of the 'pleasure room' that it was heavily scented with flowers to create an erotic ambience.

Some men think that women wash too much. At a time when people constantly seem to be hopping into the shower and our fears about body odour are reinforced by advertisements for deodorants and perfumes, you would think it unlikely that the natural scent of a woman is much sought after, yet our natural scent is an integral part of the chemistry of attraction. We can disguise it, but a potential partner will unconsciously detect it beneath the artificial scents, as we do theirs. Your reaction to the scent of someone's skin and sweat tells you the truth about your feelings for them.

Leaving your personal scent around for a man to smell when you have left is highly erotic. You could leave an item of clothing behind for example. If you have been sleeping with him, he will be able to smell you on the pillows and sheets. There is something wonderful about suddenly detecting the scent of your lover when they are not there: it transports you back to memories of pleasure.

Taste

As with smell, the taste of a lover can turn you on. Run your tongue over your lover's skin and find out what you think about him. Kiss him all over his body, bury your nose in his hair and inhale deeply. Give him a blowjob and see if you like the taste of his semen.

Food and drink have always played their parts too. The *Kama Sutra* includes them in foreplay, saying, *'They can then eat sweetmeats, drink the fresh juice of mango fruits...anything that is known to be sweet, soft and pure.'*

Plan a sensual meal and include foods that can be eaten with the fingers, such as Middle Eastern and Greek recipes like hummus and tzatziki. Set out a selection of seductive fruits like strawberries, dates, mangoes and figs. Eat food off your partner's fingers rather than a fork. Undress and let him eat food off your body. Make sure he licks you clean...

Romance

The *Kama Sutra* has much to say about successfully maintaining a sexual relationship, but it does not mention the concept of romance, because it is a relatively recent notion. What we think of as romance is included in the guidance on good relationships.

Our ideas of what is romantic are individual, although there are certain things that we all agree on: dining by candlelight, walking along the seashore by moonlight, sending flowers, leaving love notes and giving tokens of affection.

Whatever romance means to you, keeping it alive in a relationship is important. Making a gesture that you know your lover will find romantic shows them that you are thinking about them, that you want to please them and that you don't take them for granted. Complacency in a long-term relationship frequently leads to either partner feeling unappreciated.

Continuing to date your partner throughout the relationship is one way to keep romance alive. This may take some effort and imagination, but planning a special night out or a weekend away together has the effect of removing you both from the routine of your everyday life and helps to cement your bond. Being able to relax and focus completely on your lover revives emotional contact, and without other concerns there is time for sensuality: to exchange massages or sit in a Jacuzzi together. There is also time for talking over a long lunch or while sharing new parts of the world. Revisiting places you went to early on in your relationship also helps to rekindle the strong feelings you had when you first met. On anniversaries, some people like to return to the place they first met and pretend that they are meeting for the first time. This is both romantic and erotic.

Romance is also giving him something you know he dreams of. This could be a gift, or it could be something sexual. If there is something he wants to try and you have felt unsure about it, surprise him with your desire to at least try it because you love him.

Imagination plays a big part in romance, as does the ability to be silly and do things that are a little out of the ordinary. This could be anything from taking your lover to an amusement park and pretending you're teenagers again to booking a ride in a hot air balloon. It's not so much what you do as the love with which you do it that keeps romance alive.

'...making a gesture that you know your lover will find romantic shows them that you are thinking about them.'

Excitement and tension

When describing the build-up to sexual intercourse, the *Kama Sutra* advises taking time so that both lovers are as full of desire as they can be for the experience. In the section, '*Creating confidence in the girl*', it recommends that foreplay lasts for several days until his new bride is ready for sex. Similarly, when describing how to lead up to sex, it recommends that the couple spend the evening talking in the company of others until '*the woman is overcome with love and desire*'.

Building up excitement and tension is essential for a woman. Her body is a bit like a car being moved up through the gears until it's at full speed. How fast that happens depends on your initial feelings and how attuned your lover is to what turns you on.

Prolonged kissing gets things moving for many women, and its importance in foreplay cannot be underestimated. Having your neck kissed or touched is also bliss and almost always instantly arousing. As well as the obvious – the breasts and the thighs – having your belly, inner arms and backs of your knees touched is also hot. For maximum impact your lover should play with all these tenderly – stroking, blowing and kissing – before touching your genitals.

A woman's breasts require special attention, and some women can achieve orgasm just by having them stroked, kissed and sucked. You will have your own preferences: some women's breasts are so sensitive that only the gentlest touch will do, while others like rougher treatment. If it hurts, tell him. Pain is one way to turn a woman off instantly and dispel all the tension you have built up.

Foreplay is not just something that needs to be 'got through' in order to get to the main course: it's an important part of sexual pleasure that requires imagination and the desire to please your lover.

Delaying gratification

What the *Kama Sutra* has to say about excitement also applies to delayed gratification. This is perhaps the most wonderful way of building excitement and tension of all, but it is frequently ignored. Foreplay can be stretched out over a day or more, until the tension that builds up is sweetly unbearable. You can use text messages and e-mails to increase the anticipation while you're apart.

Tease him with your fingers and begin to make appeals to his sexual imagination. Of course, it may start because you want to have sex but have to go to work or to dinner with friends. Waiting is sexy and its possibilities are endless. Try this, or suggest your lover takes the lead role.

Tell your man that you will make love the following night. Say it as if tomorrow night is going to be an extra special night. If he asks you, 'Why not now?' don't answer him, just repeat that you will make love with him the following night then change the subject. Be affectionate, but remember not to get carried away no matter how passionately he kisses you. Don't allow him to touch your genitals either. Push his hand away gently if he does.

He will spend his sleeping and waking moments anticipating your lovemaking, and his imagination will do the work of physically arousing him. The following night, he will be ready and waiting for you when you walk through the door.

'...delaying gratification is perhaps the most wonderful way of building excitement and tension of all.'

Mutual arousal connects you. As your lover is touching you, make sure you keep hand contact with his body and seek out his hotspots. In this way you create a circle of energy which unites your two bodies and prepares you for the moment you unite physically.

If too much attention is focused on just one partner at a time there is a danger that the other will lose some of their feelings of arousal. Keeping each other aroused is a way of keeping pace with one another.

Use your intuition as well as your knowledge of what he likes. Let it guide your hands and your imagination. And don't be afraid to try something new. Ask him if he likes it. If he doesn't, you have discovered something about him.

'...keeping each other aroused is a way of keeping pace with one another.'

Kissing

On first meeting a new lover our eyes are immediately drawn to their lips again and again in anticipation of the first kiss. The lips part subtly and we wet them, imagining what it will be like. Once the lips touch and the kiss becomes longer and deeper we become aware of wanting more.

The *Kama Sutra* has plenty to say about kissing, which it recognizes as an essential part of foreplay that should be continued throughout lovemaking. It describes the different types of kissing at length and where kisses might be placed:

...the forehead, the eyes, the cheeks, the throat, the bosom, the breasts, the lips and the interior of the mouth.

There are four styles of kissing: moderate, contracted, pressed and soft. And there are four types of kiss:

The Straight Kiss – when the lips of two lovers are brought into direct contact.

The Bent Kiss – when the heads of two lovers are bent towards each other, and when so bent, kissing takes place.

The Turned Kiss – when one of them turns up the face of the other by holding the head and chin and then kisses the other.

The Pressed Kiss – when the lower lip is pressed with much force.

Our lips and tongues are erotic organs resembling the genitals, but unlike the genitals they do not tire so easily, meaning that kissing can continue throughout, and long after, intercourse. Kissing after climax is the perfect way to arouse your partner again, and there is within the Tantric tradition a form of kissing that you could teach your lover.

In Tantra it is believed that the woman's upper lip is connected through the nervous system to the clitoris. Ask your partner to gently suck or nibble on your upper lip if you would like to experience a very subtle form of stimulation to your clitoris.

This Tantric kiss is echoed in the *Kama Sutra* in *The Kiss of the Upper Lip*. While the man kisses the woman's upper lip, she presses against his lower lip.

Ultimately, the secret of good kissing, whatever style of kiss you use, is to keep the mouth, tongue and facial muscles relaxed. This increases your receptivity to your lover's lips and encourages that sense of drowning in your lover's kiss. Many Oriental sources concerned with sex agree that the tight-lipped kiss is a total turn-off and speaks volumes about a person's personality and sexual characteristics.

Take time to explore your lover's lips and have him explore yours: take it in turns to suck on each other's lips and tongues and enjoy the most sensual and erotic form of mutual exploration.

'...in Tantra it is believed that the woman's upper lip is connected through the nervous system to the clitoris.'

Bathing

They should bathe amidst the sounds of auspicious musical instruments...

The *Kama Sutra* mentions bathing quite frequently and emphasizes the importance of cleanliness as part of the upright citizen's daily routine. As it says in its description of the way in which lovers should begin intercourse: *'the woman will come bathed and dressed'* while at the end of sex, *'they should go separately to the washing room'*.

However, as with the Romans, bathing was also a leisure activity and men went to bath houses to be bathed and shaved – and sexually serviced – by eunuchs. It is interesting that the connection between public bathing and sex turns up in various cultures over the centuries and still exists today.

Bathing with your partner is an excellent way to relax your body before sex, and a perfect place to start arousing each other. It's also a good place to talk and wind down with a drink. Your bathroom can become a sanctuary for you both: close the door and you are in another world with the womb-like warmth of water, candlelight and soft scents.

Now wash each other slowly and carefully, using a natural sponge if you can because of the sensation and because you can squeeze it to create trickles of water over your lover's back or chest. Leave the genitals until last as this will build up sexual tension. Linger over this area, teasing your lover and masturbating him just enough to get him aroused.

Provided your feet are smooth and soft, lie back and rub your lover's penis between them or with just one foot. He can simultaneously use his big toe to rub your clitoris. This type of clitoral stimulation, in soapy water, can be extremely pleasurable as the clitoris is well lubricated. Ask him to bring you to your first climax of the evening – an orgasm in water is an experience not to be missed.

It is also an occasion for play, for splashing each other and having a laugh together, which is a great way to release tension from the body. Even if you don't proceed to making love, you have created some time for intimacy and relaxation, essential for relationship maintenance.

Bathing your lover is a way of pampering him. Within a relationship it is good to give pleasure to your partner regularly without seeking it for yourself. He should, of course, do likewise. If he is particularly stressed or tired, what better way to surprise him on his arrival home than with an invitation to step into your bathroom sanctuary, slip into the water and lie back while you sponge water over his body, telling him all the things about him that you love. Wash his hair and massage his scalp, and when he has had enough, dry him. Now, you can lead him to your bedroom, which should be warm and scented. Ask him to lie down, and massage him with specially prepared oil designed to lift mood and alleviate stress: neroli is a great stress-buster. He will feel like a king.

'...bathing with your partner is an excellent way to relax your body before sex, and a perfect place to start arousing each other.'

Handjobs

Showing a man you love his penis as much as he does will thrill him immensely. You can show him this with your mouth or with your hand. One of the advantages of the handjob is that it can be done in more places, especially public ones. The tedium of many a plane journey has been relieved with the aid of one of those blankets they so thoughtfully give you.

There are two fundamental keys to giving a handjob he will dream about: you must really want to do it – half-hearted handjobs give nobody pleasure – and you must handle his penis with the respect it deserves. Just because it gets hard doesn't mean that it can be treated roughly. Think about how you like your clitoris to be treated and show him the same sensitivity.

The next thing to pay attention to is your own hands. Our sense of touch is one of the most powerful when it comes to sexual expression, and when giving a handjob the focus is on the ability of your hands to transmit pleasure. They must be clean. Moisturizing them regularly will keep them in perfect condition for the job, and when it comes to nails they should be neatly manicured, as any rough edges could cause him damage. The length of your nails is a matter of personal preference, but for obvious reasons, when it comes to handjobs, men prefer shorter nails.

Getting yourself in a comfortable position is the next step. If you have to twist your arm or wrist in an awkward way you won't be able to focus on his pleasure. If he is sitting down, kneel in front of him between his legs – that way you can also use his legs to support your arms if they get tired. If he is lying on the bed, straddle his legs and prop his head up with pillows so he can watch you. Men are visual creatures and part of the thrill is watching you play with him. Glance up at him while you do it.

Using a good lubricant will enhance the sensations for him. Many people use saliva, but this dries out. Body lotion is a possible substitute for lubricant, but the skin soon absorbs it, so it is not as effective. And you shouldn't put anything inside your vagina that you wouldn't put into your mouth.

Lastly, there is technique. There are a variety of manoeuvres you can learn, but one of the best ways to find out how to give your man a good handjob is to watch how he plays with himself. Watching your man masturbate is incredibly exciting and you can learn a lot from it. Other than that, try using two hands instead of one, first cupping them under his testicles and then keeping your hands open in a V shape. Stroke upwards over the testicles; then move up the shaft of his penis, encircling it with both of your hands as you do so. Stroke down to his testicles again and keep repeating. It is important to play with his testicles and inner thighs when using a one-handed technique, as it considerably heightens his pleasure. Just be sure to handle with care – and don't dig your nails in.

Ask him to tell you what he likes, then put your whole heart into giving it to him.

'...showing a man you love his penis as much as he does will thrill him immensely.'

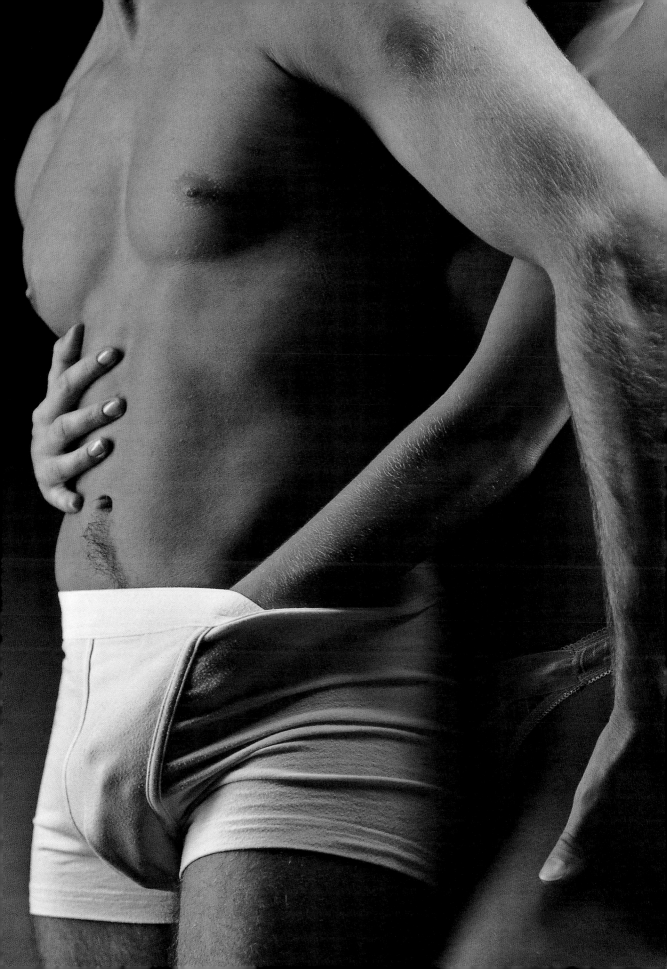

Fellatio

For a man, being taken into your mouth is the next best thing to penetrating you. It's warm, wet and soft. The only difference is that your vagina doesn't have teeth, and the first, most important, rule to giving a good blowjob is making sure you keep your teeth as far out of the way as possible. The second – as with the handjob – is to only give oral sex when you are a hundred per cent into doing it. A sensitive lover knows when you wish you were doing something else, or you're making 'to do' lists in your mind while you wait for him to come.

There are a number of reasons men love oral sex: there is slight danger involved – you have him in your mouth; and there is less emotional involvement than with intercourse. But the main appeal of the blowjob is that the man doesn't have to do anything. This is not surprising – men often feel they initiate sex more often than women do.

The *Kama Sutra* describes eight different ways of performing *'mouth congress'*. The more interesting techniques are:

Biting the sides – hold the head of the penis and lightly press your lips and teeth along the length of the shaft.
Rubbing – stroke the entire shaft and head of the penis with your tongue.
Sucking a mango fruit – place the penis halfway into your mouth and kiss and suck vigorously.
Swallowing it up – take the entire penis in the mouth and suck as if you are swallowing it.

These techniques are more or less the same as those described in some contemporary sex books. Whichever one you choose, you might want to start off by teasing him. Not every time of course, sometimes you will just want to take him in your mouth and make him come immediately. But on those longer, more languid occasions take time to use your tongue on his inner thighs, his belly button, his balls and his perineum, just behind the scrotum. He will love the feeling of his balls in your mouth, perhaps being sucked on gently one at a time.

Letting go and finding your own rhythm is essential once you've started. Think of your mouth as dancing around and up and down his penis. Think of the sensuality of belly dancing or salsa and let your mouth move like your hips. You will transmit the sensuousness to your lover and make his climax stronger. Also, if you have long hair, you can heighten the sensation for him by trailing it across his erection or by wrapping it around his shaft and using it to stroke him.

One final thing: to swallow or not to swallow? Swallowing a lover's semen can be erotic and deeply intimate; it shows him how completely you accept him. But if you do not like to swallow it does not make you a lesser lover; just tell him beforehand in a considerate way. You might also ask him if he'd like to come over your belly or your breasts. This can be as exciting for both of you as him coming in your mouth.

'...for a man, being taken into your mouth is the next best thing to penetrating you. It's warm, wet and soft.'

Not all, but many men adore going down on a woman. Indeed, some claim to love it so much that they are happy to do it all night. If you have a lover who devotes time to taking you through several climaxes, you will know the delights of having a man pay your vulva that much attention while you immerse yourself in your body. It is wonderful to know your lover's mouth is so close to your clitoris. Waves of orgasm pulse through his body and your juices flow onto his lips.

In the ancient Eastern traditions the vulva was considered a sacred part of the body. The *Kama Sutra* doesn't ignore this way of giving women pleasure and sexual satisfaction. Given that the majority of women cannot climax with penetration and thrusting alone, this is the main way in which a man can ensure his lover comes. There is manual stimulation, but if you are not wet enough, or he is a bit heavy-handed, this can be quite painful. Cunnilingus can last longer too, because the tongue is much softer than the fingers and is lubricated.

The *Kama Sutra* recommends the following:

Now spread, indeed cleave asunder, that archway with your nose and let your tongue gently probe her yoni (vagina), with your nose, lips and chin slowly circling: it becomes The Circling Tongue.

Another technique is:

Place your darling on the couch, set her feet to your shoulders, clasp her waist, suck hard and let your tongue stir her overflowing love-temple.

Lovely. Tongue circling and tracing patterns with the tip of the tongue over and around the clitoris feels very good. Working around the perineum area is also exciting and can make a woman climax fast. Sometimes encourage your lover not to allow you to come immediately. If he feels you are going to, he only has to stop for a brief second for the tension to subside. Then he can build it up again. You will probably find that when your lover uses this technique, you will experience very deep, strong orgasms and are more likely to climax two or more times in quick succession.

After you have climaxed, it is nice to have your lover stay there for a little while, keeping his mouth still against your clitoris. If you've had a very strong orgasm, the aftershock of it can make you feel over-sensitive around your clitoris, and his mouth or hand there helps to calm the nerve endings down. Ask your lover to kiss you on the mouth after you've climaxed so that you can taste and smell your own juices. Apart from the pleasure of your scent and finding his mouth so warm and wet, it will increase your confidence about your vulva: that it really does taste good and is a beautiful thing.

Take some pictures of it if you are less than comfortable with the image you have of it. Men are a great deal more appreciative of women's genitals than we are. Maybe you should ask him to tell you how it appears to him.

'...in the ancient Eastern traditions the vulva was considered a sacred part of the body.'

Objects for arousal

There are hundreds of objects of arousal catering to all tastes: sex toys, porn films and magazines, erotic verse and short stories, Japanese pillow books, fruit, ice cubes, ice cream, scarves, stockings, the list is endless. Even the *Kama Sutra* says that in the room you make love in you should have *'...books containing amorous songs with illustrations of love postures'* and, as we know, it describes the courtesans using vegetables and the male genitals on statues to masturbate themselves. Sex toys, especially the dildo, existed in most ancient civilizations, so men and women have always added to the pleasure given by hands, mouth and penis. Primarily, using objects to help arouse you both is a way to play and stimulate your imagination. Both help your emotional health.

Women are no longer afraid to enter sex shops and buy what they want. There are even 'women only' sex shops, and internet shopping has meant that women can experiment without worrying if they are going to bump into somebody they know. Knowing what to buy can be daunting: faced with a huge variety of dildos and vibrators, how do you choose? Do you want a hard vibrator, or a soft jelly-like one? There are some exquisite glass dildos available if you want to really splash out – some women may prefer to insert a non-vibrating dildo in their vagina while using a tiny clit

vibrator at the same time. What's the difference between all of these anyway? This is where being in a women-only store makes an incredible difference: ask an assistant to talk you through the different types and their features.

It's best to have a selection of vibrators if possible. Then you can experiment with them and use them according to how you are feeling. The basic vibrator is straight and smooth. Then there are small, soft vibrators (the jelly type for example) which are bent so that you can stimulate the G-spot and the clitoris at the same time. Some women prefer the type that look like a penis: these are somewhere between hard and soft and satisfy the need to have something 'realistic' to play with. The one that most people know and love is the Rabbit, with its ears that stimulate the clitoris while the head vibrates inside the vagina.

While you are at the sex store, buy some lubricant – this will really get things going. If you like anal play then you could try anal beads. Care is always needed when inserting anything into the anus and you should inspect any product carefully for rough edges. If you are sharing it with your lover, cover it with a condom each time it is used.

Enjoy your exploration of the sex toy world if you haven't already, and create an adult toy chest.

'...using objects to help arouse you both is a way to play and stimulate your imagination.'

Dressing up, dressing down

'...today's women are giving men a preview of what lies beneath.'

Fantasy wear

Dressing up for sex seems like a contradiction in terms, yet if we are to play out our fantasies it helps enormously: it is difficult to create a believable harem dancer in jeans and T-shirt. Of course, the author of the *Kama Sutra* hadn't encountered a nurse's uniform. What is more, Vatsyayana, being a man, didn't even pick up on the fact that girls like dressing up.

You can create your own fantasy wear, or take a trip to a sex store or fetish wear fair and discover the amazing range of clothes available for every taste and fantasy. The classic French maid's outfit and nurse's uniform are available in most places, but if you want something a little more out of the ordinary you might want to try one of the women-only sex shops, which tend to have broader and better-quality ranges than the ones for both men and women. Alternatively, the Internet can provide easy, hassle-free shopping.

One of the key aspects of fantasy wear is that it should be as different as possible from your usual style of dress. That way you can get into the fantasy and leave your everyday self behind; this has the effect of liberating you from your usual sexual behaviour – if you are 'not you' then you can do anything you want, try things that you would be afraid to at other times. In some ways, fantasy wear is a way of administering your own sex therapy.

Dressing up may feel a bit silly at first, but once you get over the initial fear of making a fool of yourself, you will find it brings immeasurable rewards. Your partner will love watching you perform for him, whether you are a geisha, a belly dancer or Little Red Riding Hood discovering the Big Bad Wolf. Physical sensations are heightened during fantasy sex too, which will encourage you to repeat the experience.

If you don't want to splash out on specialist fantasy wear until you've experimented with different roles, it is easy enough to create some outfits from clothes you already have. Scarves in all lengths and textures are essential and, like stockings, can perform all sorts of other functions. Long beaded necklaces can also add to an outfit and be used to tease your lover. Chain belts, sarongs, kimonos and other items might all be lurking in your wardrobe just waiting for an alternative use.

Shoes are another vital item – men love to look at legs in extremely high heels and it is worth having a pair just for play: even if you could never walk down the road in them. Unfortunately, women in the *Kama Sutra* didn't have access to this type of footwear and probably had to rely on the eroticism of the bare foot.

Once you have created your homemade outfits you might feel brave enough to move on to more exotic erotic wear, such as rubber and leather.

'...one of the key aspects of fantasy wear is that it should be as different as possible from your usual style of dress.'

Many people are afraid of wearing rubber. It has strong associations with sado-masochism – particularly gimp suits, those frightening outfits which encase the whole body including the face. More practically, others are put off by the fact that you have to cover yourself in talcum powder to get them on, that they're not ideal in the heat and that they reveal every bump and bulge. Still, they're very sexy.

The skin-like look and texture of rubber, the sense of slipperiness that it gives is part of its attraction and its sexiness. For the wearer, the tightness creates tension that makes them more aware of their body and enhances feelings of arousal.

PVC is a good alternative to rubber and is much easier to get on. Its shiny surface and the way it encases the body signals tension and restriction which is arousing. There are some fabulous PVC dresses available from most sex shops or fetish clothing shops that you could wear in public if you feel like tantalizing your lover. And there are some equally cute PVC outfits that you might not wear outside the bedroom.

However, if you want to feel really dangerous there is a much better fabric to wear...

Nothing says 'I'm feeling sexy' like leather. A good-fitting pair of leather trousers can make you feel like a big cat on the prowl and look good regardless of your age. In fact, the older a woman is, the stronger the sexual message given out. Of course, some restraint is needed: head-to-toe leather outfits in pink or white, for example, have none of the potency of a pair of plain black leather trousers.

Leather is sexy because it comes from an animal. Being clothed in leather lends you an animal vibe, which can be a real turn-on for a lot of people. When your lover strokes your leather-clad leg, it stirs up primal urges and images of cavemen clothed only in skins. It is primarily skin on skin, and feeling it next to yours can be deeply erotic, akin to lying naked, wrapped in furs.

Many women feel that only thin women with long legs can get away with wearing leather trousers. However, this is just a fashion myth. Go and try a pair on, if only to get an idea of how they look. See if they don't make you feel sexy and ready to strut your stuff.

'...the skin-like look and texture of rubber, the sense of slipperiness that it gives

is part of its attraction and its sexiness.'

Masks and accessories

The Venetians have known about the eroticism of masks for centuries. If you want to understand the sexual thrill of wearing a mask, try visiting Venice during carnival in February. Buy a mask while you're there.

Masks are for hiding behind, and for creating illusions. Imagine being at a masked ball centuries ago and the flirtations between people well known to each other whose identities were concealed behind the mask.

Masks, like fantasy wear, also allow us to envelop ourselves in other identities, perhaps an aspect of our sexuality that we are unsure about but which we would like to explore. They also make the onlooker focus on the eyes in order to understand what the person is feeling.

You could create a mask with face paints or make-up, combining it with your fantasy wardrobe. In fact, painting on a mask will make the transformation complete and should remove the fear of looking foolish. Experiment with different looks – fierce as well as seductive and feminine. Do it just for yourself and see how you feel when you are 'in character'. Then reveal all these different aspects of yourself to your man.

Striptease

You're going to be his private dancer – he won't believe his luck! You've sat him down with a drink, and maybe even rearranged the room so he seems to be sitting at a club table. You dim the lights or light the room with candles. So far it's an ordinary evening. You have dressed up and he likes what you're wearing, then you leave the room to get something. He hears you coming back, but suddenly out of nowhere there's some familiar music: it's The Stripper.

You enter the room swinging your hips provocatively and circle in front of him. You undo a button, you turn away and wiggle your hips at him, and when you turn round again, your top is undone. Taking it slowly you proceed from there, never getting close enough for him to touch you, until you're down to your G-string, when you can play with it right in front of his face. Will you, won't you take it off? Delay it as long as you can then ask him to remove it without using his hands – which means he has to use his teeth and lips. Now, as he removes it he can take a few moments to pleasure you with his tongue, if you can restrain him from penetrating you for long enough.

Using accessories such as feather boas or silky scarves to cover your breasts and other parts of you can also be incredibly sexy as you slowly reveal yourself.

Practise this by yourself until your movements have the kind of flow a professional stripper achieves – they don't fumble over buttons or fall over removing a skirt. Having said that, your lover will appreciate you being his personal stripper/lap dancer, however you perform. Anyway, once you get down to the G-string it's up to him to help you!

'...masks are for hiding behind and for creating illusions.'

Going the whole way

The *Kama Sutra* is synonymous with sexual postures, indeed most people know little else about what it has to say. What follow are the main postures of the *Kama Sutra*, offering you a menu that ranges from the vigorous, athletic and physically passionate to the soft and intimate.

We tend to get stuck in a sexual rut when it comes to the positions in which we have sex. This doesn't mean that every time you have sex you have to engage in a series of athletic postures in order to prove that your sex life is exciting. However, sexual positions are like different foods: you won't know if you like each one until you try it.

Women are often more adventurous than men and more up for getting out of the Missionary position and into new postures. The parallel between experimentation in the bedroom and in the kitchen is an interesting one and brings to mind the Dalai Lama's recommendation that one should 'approach love and cooking with reckless abandon'. Sex is nurturing in the way that food is. So, if you care about the food you put in your body, you should also care about the quality of the sex you have.

As for the positions, there are fewer woman on top postures than you might expect – the *Kama Sutra* actually provides very few. Still, there are other postures described here that give the woman total control while either sitting, lying sideways or lying on her back.

What I have tried to provide are postures that you can alternate – perhaps from the vigorous to the restful – and ones that encourage you to get in touch with your female sexual energy and increase your appreciation of it in order to use it to your advantage. Of course, pleasure is the main aim and I hope that all of the postures, even the more strenuous ones, will bring you that. I hope also that many will help you to experience orgasm while being penetrated: something that many women would admit to needing a little help with.

'...sexual positions are like different foods: you won't know if you like each one until you try it.'

The plough

Rear entry postures should be as erotic for you as they are for him. For the man much of the pleasure is visual, while for the woman the physical sensations play a greater part.

Why it's great for women

The Plough allows you the freedom to move your hips in ways that increase your pleasure, while the man has more control over his thrusting. Ask him to start shallow and slow and alternate this with deep and fast thrusts, varying the speed and depth according to both his and your enjoyment. Physiologically, the shallow thrusts create a vacuum in the vagina and the deep thrusts force the air out, which adds to the woman's pleasure. Added to this, when thrusting is varied there is a better chance of stimulating the G-spot. Finally, this position vastly increases the woman's chance of achieving orgasm during penetration because the man, or the woman herself, can play with her clitoris.

What to do

Your lover kneels while you sit astride his lap, facing away from him. You then bend forward in a prayer-like posture until you are at an angle where he can enter you. Now stretch one leg back, alongside his, while keeping the other bent, and rest your arms and head on pillows.

   An easier, more relaxed version of this posture is The Elephant (see pages 78–79). You can move into this from The Plough if you feel less energetic.

'...this position allows you the freedom to move your hips in ways that increase your pleasure.'

The *Kama Sutra* considers thrusting an art form and provides a detailed 'system' of thrusting called Sets of Nine, devised with positions like The Plough in mind. Men are instructed to repeat as many sets as possible before climaxing. Encourage your man to learn this system and use it yourself when you are in a woman-on-top posture.

This posture is sexy because it is animal yet sensual. Some women prefer positions where you can look at each other. If you are one of these – turn to face him.

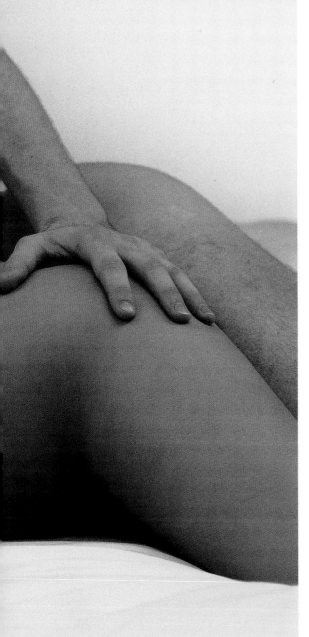

The elephant

If you find you're feeling the strain of being in The Plough posture this curiously named position is perfect for relaxation.

Why it's great for women
First, not only is it relaxing but it allows for deep penetration, too. You can choose whether your lover uses gentle or strong movements, and as with The Plough, good G-spot stimulation is likely.

Also, it's good for taking a rest without him losing his erection. Let your lover lie along your back and, staying still, use your internal muscles to stroke him. If he feels he's getting soft, you stay still and let him tease you with some shallow thrusting until he's hard again. Alternating this kind of complete stillness with some more vigorous thrusting can help you to achieve orgasm with your lover inside you. You can also help things along by rubbing yourself against whatever you are lying on. Alternatively, slip your hand underneath your belly and place the tips of your fingers over your clitoris.

What to do
If you have started off in The Plough posture, you can try moving into this position without your lover withdrawing. If you find it difficult to do this without him slipping out, get him to place a cushion under your pelvis as you drop down from the kneeling position. As you move down to the bed, you may want to put cushions beneath your breasts and head so that you can relax completely. Your lover then supports himself with one hand on the bed or on your hip, so that his body is lying along yours but you are not taking any of his weight.

'...this position is relaxing and allows for deep penetration, too.'

Congress of a cow

For a complete contrast to the two preceding rear entry
postures, this standing posture is ideal for use outside
the bedroom and when you feel like some fast sex.

Why it's great for women
Imagine you both have the sudden urge to have sex
in the kitchen. With this posture you don't have to
undress completely to get into it, you can just pull
your trousers down or lift up your skirt so that your
lover can enter you. You could use a kitchen stool
to balance against, or if you are in another room, you
could use the arm of a sofa or back of an armchair.
Traditionally, this posture requires the woman to bend
over completely so that she is touching her feet,
completely exposing her genitals for the man to see,
but for most people this is uncomfortable – and if your
body feels strained you'll miss the point, which is to
enjoy the pleasure.

   Fast sex is good for your relationship: being
spontaneous keeps passion alive for long-term lovers.
The author of the *Kama Sutra* recognized that passion
can arise quickly and that sometimes it should also
be satisfied quickly.

What to do
You bend over as far as is comfortable for you and
support yourself on a stool, chair or whatever is nearest
to hand. Your lover enters you from behind and clasps
you around the waist, wrapping his arms right round
you. As you are supported by him, this allows you to
join in the thrusting movements with him, moving your
hips back towards him as he thrusts into you.

'...fast sex is good for your relationship:

being spontaneous keeps passion

alive for long-term lovers.'

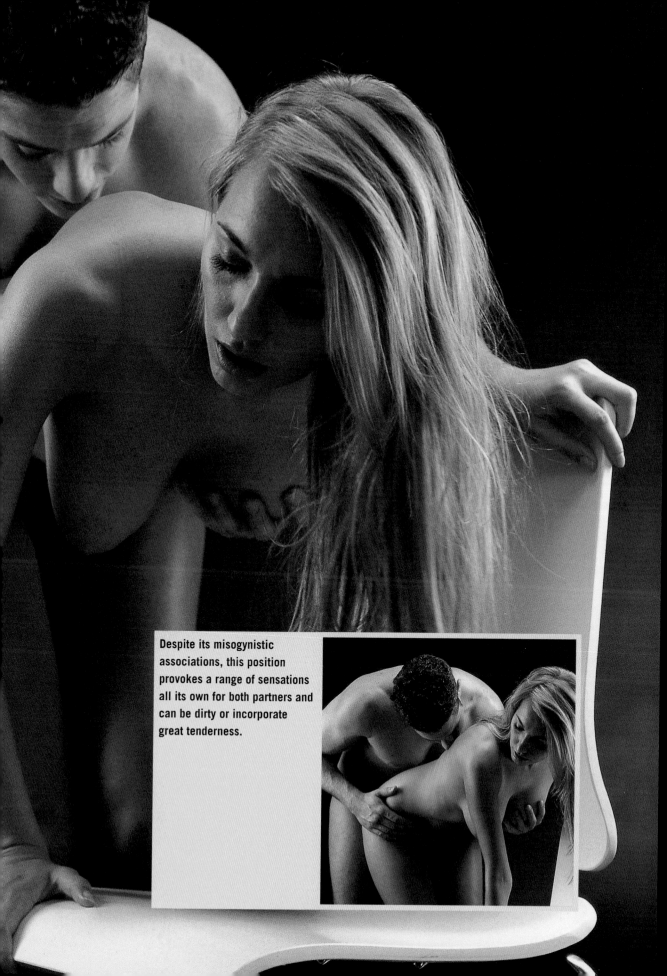

Despite its misogynistic associations, this position provokes a range of sensations all its own for both partners and can be dirty or incorporate great tenderness.

Eternal bliss

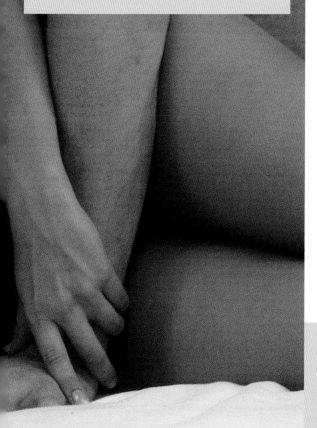

This is lovely because it is more like a story or a dance than a posture. In its slow, deliberate, loving way, it optimizes on the drama of lovemaking.

Even the author of the *Kama Sutra* knew that sex is one of best ways to make up after an argument or to become reacquainted after time apart. This rear entry posture was originally devised to represent the reunion of lovers after a long separation, when the anticipation of sex is heightened. The movements are slow and tender, and the posture is relaxing for languorous lovemaking.

Why it's great for women

It is a very graceful pose which allows you to keep in touch with your femininity. There is an intimacy and softness about this posture which is emotionally comforting for a woman as, when fully in the posture, your body is cradled by the man. You can also use your imagination with it and create the effect of being in the harem, lying on a couch waiting for your lover. You could use diaphanous scarves, exotically covered cushions, and incense or aromatic oils to complete the effect.

What to do

Enter into this pose thinking seductively. Sit on the floor with your legs together, stretched out but slightly bent, and your head turned away from your body, looking back over your shoulder. If you wish, put a pile of cushions between your supporting arm and your body so that you can lie on them later. Your lover kneels at your feet and strokes them. As he does this you half turn towards him, inviting him to come closer. Your lover then moves his body up along your back, stroking and kissing it until he is able to embrace your shoulders and reach over to kiss your mouth. You then roll over more onto your side so that he can enter you from behind. Once inside he can curl his body around yours.

'...use your imagination and create the effect of being in the harem, lying on a couch waiting for your lover.'

The flying white tiger

This is another seductive rear entry posture that is more energetic and focuses on deep penetration.

Why it's great for women

Like Eternal Bliss, this posture encourages you to use your powers of seduction. You could start this posture half-dressed and use your clothing to tease him, edging your underwear down to show him how aroused you are. This should encourage him to turn into the Flying White Tiger and leap onto you, entering you with the urgency you desire. Again this is an ideal posture for G-spot stimulation, and although you won't have much movement, due to the man clasping you tightly towards his body, you can tell him how deep and fast to thrust.

What to do

While your lover watches you from behind, arrange yourself in a comfortable kneeling position. Make sure that you wriggle your rear seductively for him as you get into position, and if you are still wearing underwear, pull it down slowly. Be aware of your lover getting aroused watching your body movements.

Now you are in a comfortable position, supported by your forearms and the pillows under your upper body, your lover kneels behind you and enters you immediately. He clasps you around the waist and pulls you back onto his penis, penetrating you deeply. Ideally he should use a mixture of deep and shallow thrusting as this will prolong your pleasure. Although you will be unable to touch your clitoris, you should be able to rub yourself against one of the pillows to help you climax.

Another predatory posture, this allows you to indulge your coquettish side. It also enables him to penetrate you deeply – although if he is clever he will mix deep thrusts with shallow ones to tip you over the edge.

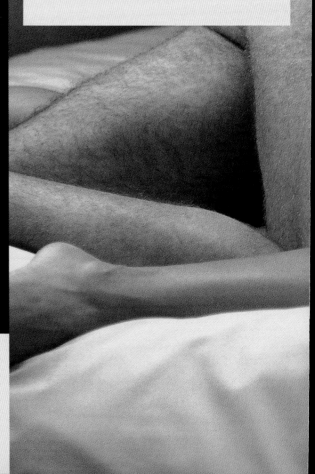

'...tantalize your lover with a view of your rear as you arrange yourself in the position.'

Parvati's dance

This posture is named after the Hindu goddess most associated with sensuality and the celebration of womanhood.

Why it's great for women

Any woman-on-top position gives you control over both the pleasure you give your lover and the pleasure you experience yourself. It's also an opportunity to let your lover lie back and watch you enjoy yourself and the gratification that his body can bring you, which will heighten his pleasure. This posture allows you to express your passion for your lover in a very sexy way.

In this posture you use circular movements of the hips rather than an up and down motion. Within various Eastern traditions this is seen as being good for increasing your sexual energy, which is why so many Eastern dance moves feature rapid, circular hip movements.

What to do

Your lover lies on his back, either on a bed or on soft coverings on the floor. You may prefer the stability of the floor as it will help you to keep your balance.

You then stand over his thighs, your legs on either side of his. Squatting down over him, guide his penis into you. Support yourself by reaching behind you and placing your hands on his calves. Now squeeze your legs tightly together, your knees meeting over his belly.

In this position you rotate your waist and hips, changing direction when you want to. As you swivel your hips round throw your head back and swing your hair around. If you find it difficult to balance in this squatting position, try interlacing your fingers with your lover's, pushing against his palms to steady yourself.

Perhaps the ultimate posing posture for a woman. And you get to use those sexy circular movements which, with thrusting, can produce a very satisfactory effect indeed.

'...this posture allows you to express your passion for your lover in a very sexy way.'

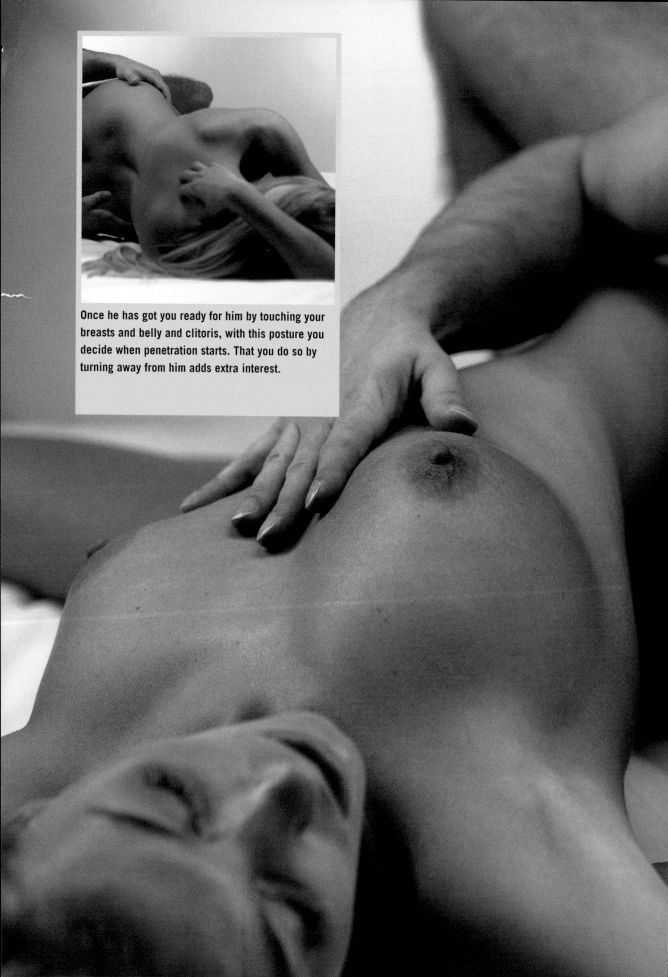

Once he has got you ready for him by touching your breasts and belly and clitoris, with this posture you decide when penetration starts. That you do so by turning away from him adds extra interest.

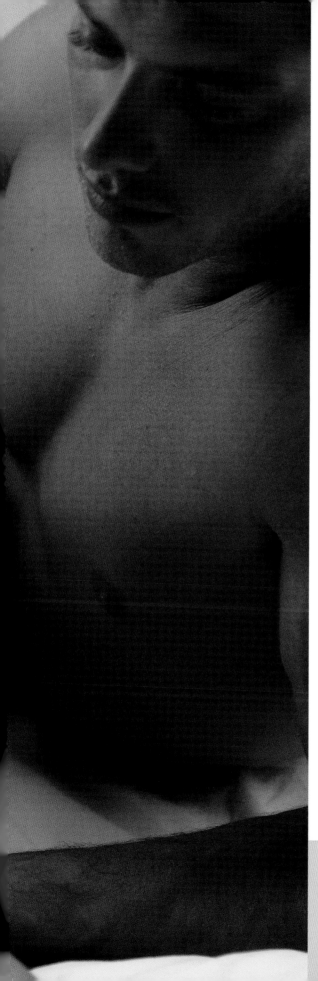

The path of life

This slightly more difficult rear entry posture is wonderful for leisurely stimulation before penetration. It is not a posture for women with back problems.

Why it's great for women

You will need to be fairly flexible to enjoy this posture, and the stronger your back is the better. Having said that, it is a posture that begins in a very leisurely fashion with your lover stroking your breasts and stimulating your clitoris. Once you start to get into the position, one of its many benefits is that it offers a slightly unusual angle of entry for the penis and your lover can continue playing with your breasts and clitoris while thrusting. Penetration will not be too deep, but the G-spot will be stimulated.

What to do

Your lover lies on his right side with his right leg bent in front of him. You lie on your back with your legs bent at the knees and draped over his right leg. He holds you around the shoulders with his right arm and with his left he strokes your breasts and clitoris while you kiss. When you want him to penetrate you, turn your back away from him and stretch your right leg out straight, placing it between his legs, at the same time tilting your upper body forwards towards his right knee. Now he can enter you. Once he is in, he pulls your upper body back towards him, so that your back is almost flat on the bed again. Then he hooks his right ankle under your left knee to anchor your leg to the bed. As you turn your face towards him to kiss him again, he clutches your right knee with his left hand and draws it backwards.

'...if you can get into this position you may discover a whole new range of sensations.'

A pair of flying ducks

This woman-on-top position offers an interesting alternative to the typical posture in that you face away from the man. In fact it is a little like a combination of woman on top and rear entry.

Why it's great for women

Sometimes it's good to be able to become absorbed in the sensations you are experiencing during sex without having to communicate directly with your partner. This position offers you a way of giving yourself pleasure while knowing that your partner is not excluded. As with rear entry postures, he has the excitement of watching your body move on his. It also allows you to play with your clitoris while being penetrated and is an excellent posture for any woman who has difficulty climaxing with her lover inside her. This is very common, but if you can masturbate yourself without inhibition while he is penetrating you, it will become easier to climax like this in time.

What to do

Your lover lies on his back with his legs together while you kneel astride him facing his feet. Raising yourself up, put his penis inside you, then gently lower yourself back down. You could at this point tease him by only taking him in little by little. You can now stroke your clitoris and breasts while your lover plays with your buttocks and your back. Vary your movements to keep him erect and use your vaginal muscles to stimulate both of you. If you like to be watched, doing this in front of a mirror adds another dimension, because your lover can see you play with yourself.

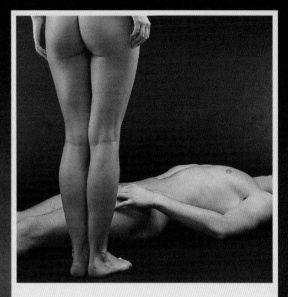

Take control of the lovemaking and of stimulating yourself. He can close his eyes and let you take him over or open them and enjoy a great view of you from behind.

'...this position offers you a way of giving yourself pleasure while knowing that your partner is not excluded.'

The Lotus flower has had all sorts of symbolic meanings, among them fertility and the triumph of the spirit over the senses. This elegant posture allows intimacy and space at the same time.

Lotus

In this slightly unconventional pose you can either fall asleep or keep your lover inside you after his climax, using your vaginal muscles to arouse him again.

Why it's great for women

This posture can be used in a number of ways. It can be used to stay close after passionate sex or it can be used as a pause during lovemaking. A woman may find it particularly appealing, as she can bring herself to climax while her lover rests and watches her. This is quite a turn-on for men, yet it is something a woman is frequently nervous about doing in case her partner feels he is not enough for her. Instead, it may be the trigger for a renewed bout of passion. This posture is also a meditative pose, providing the stillness of the Tantric tradition in which you focus your attention on how your body is feeling and how your senses are affected by the closeness of your lover, with only minimum body contact.

What to do

Your lover sits on the bed with his left leg stretched out in front of him and his right leg slightly bent, his foot flat on the bed. He places his hands behind him to support himself. You sit facing him, placing your left leg below his right leg and your right leg over his left. If you want penetration, ask your lover to enter you now. If not, lean back on your hands for support. Reach out with your right hand to grasp your lover's right arm, each of you still leaning on one elbow. Now both of you lower yourselves backwards onto the bed, and you can extend your legs on either side of your lover.

'...after a vigorous lovemaking session it's good to find a posture you can totally relax in.'

Yab yum

Sitting postures are fun and can be energetic or restful. They are also good for kissing and talking, and can be used without penetration or to arouse your lover.

Why it's great for women

In general, sitting postures are great for helping a woman to focus on the sensations in her genitals and become more aware of how different movements alter them. Adopting this posture without penetration, you can sense how the closeness of your lover's genitals to yours creates sensation. By focusing on this sensation you will find that you can increase your arousal without your lover touching you, or you touching yourself. This is like advanced masturbation and will enhance your ability to climax with ease.

What to do

This is a floor posture and you will need to put a soft quilt or a large floor cushion down for you to sit on. Your partner may also want something supporting his back but it is possible to be comfortable in this posture without support.

   Your lover sits with his legs apart. This is more comfortable than the cross-legged position recommended in the *Kama Sutra*. You then sit astride his legs and wrap your legs around his back, and your arms around his neck. If your lover is erect you can help him to enter you immediately. If you are using this position to arouse him and yourself, you can make circular or sideways motions with your hips until you are both sufficiently excited. This is a good posture for a prolonged kissing session or for exchanging fantasies and talking intimately.

'...this is like advanced masturbation and will enhance your ability to climax with ease.'

The swing

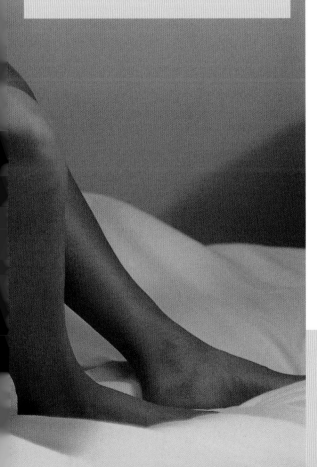

Tiny variations can make all the difference to this loving posture. You may well find that the rocking sensation arouses both of you in a new and heady way.

This sitting posture is a perfect follow-on from Yab Yum as it requires little change in position. In fact, using these two together will allow you to alternate movement with stillness, prolonging your lovemaking.

Why it's great for women
In Yab Yum you are able to build up your arousal before penetration. You may find that once you have reached the point where you want to be penetrated you will naturally move from Yab Yum into The Swing posture, as you want a more intense feeling of having your lover inside you. The Swing is a great way of achieving climax without other forms of stimulation, as your clitoris is directly stimulated by being rubbed along the shaft of your lover's penis. It is also a great posture if you find deep penetration painful at any time.

What to do
As with Yab Yum your lover sits with his legs falling open. You then sit between them, rather than on his lap. Again, make sure you have plenty of soft coverings on the floor or this posture will become uncomfortable for you both. Place your legs around his back with your feet firmly resting on the floor. Hold your lover around his neck while he holds you around your lower back. At this point your lover should enter you. You may need to help each other and alter your posture until he is inside you, after which you can hold each other as described. Both of you then use the weight of your bodies to rock back and forth. You might start off with gentle movements and then combine them with much stronger ones. This will vary the sensation, giving you a good chance of reaching orgasm.

'...this position is a great way of achieving climax without other forms of stimulation.'

The swallow

This posture, which is a variation on the classic Missionary, encourages a very deep penetration not always possible with face-to-face positions.

Why it's great for women

In this posture you can vary the position of your legs and buttocks to control the depth of penetration. As you alter your leg positions, you alter the shape of your vagina. So, for example, raising your legs higher shortens and tightens the vagina, making it fit more snugly around the penis. This is also a good pose to practise your communication skills in, as your lover has control over movement and you will need to tell him when to vary the depth and rhythm of his thrusting. Deep penetration can be painful for some women for a variety of reasons. Don't feel you have to put up with it if you're not enjoying it.

What to do

You lie on your back with a pillow supporting your head. Draw your knees up towards your chest and hold them there. Having an arousing full view of your genitals, your lover approaches you in this pose and kneels in front of you, holding your feet up for you. He then helps you put your feet on his shoulders. Now he penetrates you and supports himself with his hands to either side of your hips. If having your feet on his shoulders is uncomfortable, try either placing your feet under his armpits, or get him to place one or two pillows under your hips until you feel comfortable.

Within reason, it is sexy for your partner to move your body around during sex – make sure he knows this. Perhaps start The Swallow slowly to get the depth of penetration right.

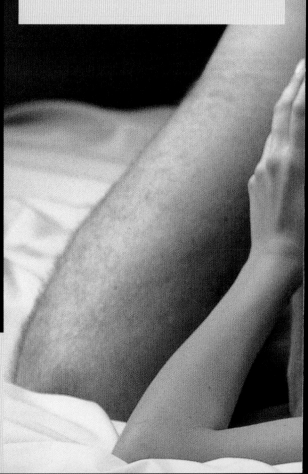

'...in this posture you can vary the position of your legs and buttocks to control the depth of penetration.'

Splitting the bamboo

This posture complements The Swallow and together they are ideal for using alternately, as one gives control to the man and the other to the woman.

Why it's great for women

Splitting the Bamboo gives you total control over movement and the sensations you experience while lying on your back. In this respect it is fairly unique, as in most supine postures women have very little control. Your lover will appreciate you taking charge as it relieves him of the burden of feeling responsible for creating sexual pleasure. If you vary the pace of your movements between energetic and slow you can create an erotic dance-like rhythm that will increase the pleasure for both of you. One addition you could make is to hold a vibrator over your clitoris in this posture. This will help both of you climax.

What to do

You lie on your back on the bed, or on cushions on the floor. Your lover kneels in front of you. Stretch out one of your legs and place it on his shoulder. Your other leg you bend back towards your chest and place your foot on his chest. Your lover then moves in towards you and places his knees to either side of your hips. He should then be able to enter you. Now you alternate the positions of your legs, which being quite close together make the vagina tight around the penis. The movements of your legs massage the penis and keep him erect while he remains still. If you feel tired, and want your lover to take over for a while, keep your legs still and let him thrust into you.

'...you can create an exotic dance-like rhythm that will increase the pleasure for both of you.'

Padmini

This is a more restful variation on Splitting the Bamboo, and as with other positions that have similarities, you may want to alternate between them.

Why it's great for women

In this posture the vagina is shortened and tightened. This makes it ideal for your lover to tease you with some very shallow thrusting. Of course, you may not need to ask him, he may know already that only allowing the head of the penis to enter the vagina will drive you wild until you beg him to thrust in hard and deep.

Because the vagina is tightened you may find that it helps to use some lubricant before your lover enters you. Using lubricant does not signal lack of desire, although some men seem to think this. Rather, using a lubricant significantly heightens your sensations, so it's a good idea to find one that you like the texture and smell of.

What to do

You lie on your back and pull your knees up to your chest, gripping your knees to hold them together. Your lover, having a full view of your vulva again, kneels in front of you with his knees to either side of your hips. You rest your feet on his solar plexus. Your lover can now tease you with shallow thrusts, perhaps also stimulating your clitoris manually if you would like him to. This is another ideal posture in which your lover can use the 'Sets of Nine' style of thrusting described in the *Kama Sutra* (see page 77). Also, for your lover, this posture allows him to see his penis plunging in and out of you, which greatly adds to his pleasure.

'...this is an ideal posture for your lover to tease you with some very shallow thrusting.'

Wild abandon

This energetic posture does require a degree of suppleness and strength, and you may not be able to stay in the position for long. If you have lower back problems or tight hamstrings, it may be better not to attempt it. Yoga, which the original readers of the *Kama Sutra* would have been familiar with, is perfect for getting your body into shape for Wild Abandon.

Why it's great for women

Sex is about pleasure but it is also great exercise for women and so much more fun than the gym. If you are comfortable in this posture, and able to sustain it for some time, you should experience the pleasure of deep penetration and both clitoral and G-spot stimulation which will swiftly bring you to orgasm.

What to do

Your lover sits upright on the floor with his legs stretched out in front of him. He may need the edge of the bed or sofa to support his back. You kneel astride him, facing him. He penetrates you and you wrap your arms around each other. Letting go of him, you lean back while he supports you by holding your waist until you can support yourself by placing your hands behind you on his legs. Now swing your right leg up and over his left shoulder. Once you feel steady, your lover places his hands behind him to support himself. Using this support he raises his buttocks off the ground to thrust into you as hard as he can. His thrusting movements will lift your body with his, although you always keep one foot on the ground for support. When you want to rest, remove your leg from his shoulder and hold each other tightly.

If you are strong and flexible, this is a good, dynamic posture. You will need to get your acts together, though – you are balancing on just one foot and him. Practise and mind your back...

'...this energetic posture is for when your bodies have warmed up.'

Yin yang

After the exertions of Wild Abandon you will probably want to relax completely. This beautiful posture allows you to do just that while keeping intimate contact.

Why it's great for women

You can completely relax and your lower back is well supported because your legs are draped over his hips. If you adopt this position just after orgasm, when your lover is still relatively hard, you can lie still and stroke his penis with your vaginal muscles, keeping him inside you for as long as possible. If he hasn't climaxed yet, you can use the same technique to keep him hard until you feel like adopting another position where he can thrust again. It's also a good position to take a little nap in, especially if the weather is warm and you don't need to cover up.

What to do

Your lover lies on his side across the bed either resting his head on his hand or on a pillow so that he can stretch his arm out. He is less likely to get pins and needles this way. Lie back at right angles to him and drape your legs over his hips. Your lover can then hold your legs and fondle them, while with his other hand he holds yours. If you want him to penetrate you, guide him into you now and use your vaginal muscles to keep him erect. Just feeling his penis near your vulva can also be exciting; let the tension that this creates arouse you all by itself.

'...this beautiful posture allows you
to relax completely while keeping
intimate contact.'

Yawning posture

There is nothing boring about this position: yawning here is in the sense of being wide open.

Why it's great for women

This is a pose in which you give control to your lover. It is a good exercise emotionally for a woman because it helps you to understand the process of giving and receiving. Having said that, you can participate in it by using your vaginal muscles to pleasure your partner. The more you use these, the more toned they will become, which is a great health benefit for women and helps you to enjoy sex a lot more. As you remain completely still in this posture, it is great for any woman who finds it difficult to move her hips while on her back, or who has lower back problems.

What to do

You lie on your back with your head supported by a pillow. Spread your legs out to either side as far as is comfortable for you. Your lover kneels in front of you spreading his knees apart so they are either side of your hips. Keeping your legs straight and wide open, with your toes pointed, rest your legs on top of his thighs. Your lover penetrates you and supports himself on his hands, which are placed either side of you. As he is in control of thrusting, tell him what you want. If you find it too tiring to keep your legs straight, you can vary your posture by crossing them around his back or bending them at the knees. If you like the latter you could ask your lover to hold your legs behind the knees otherwise your feet are likely to drop down onto the bed.

'...this is a pose in which you give control to your lover.'

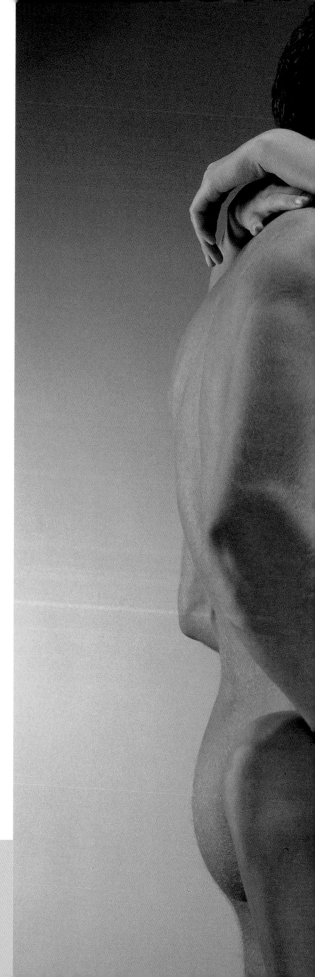

The three footprints

This posture from the *Kama Sutra* is one of the simpler standing poses, which everyone can perform.

Why it's great for women

Standing postures are great for fast sex, and if you are wearing a dress or skirt you can achieve it without undressing. This is excellent for when a woman wants to take the initiative in sex, which is always pleasing for a man. Perhaps you want him as soon as he comes through the door? Pin him up against the wall, kiss him passionately and get him aroused quickly. Unzip him and get him erect, then ask him to help you get into this posture. If you're a lot shorter than him you may not be able to keep one foot on the floor, but by using the stairs you may be able to even things up so that he can enter you.

What to do

Stand facing your lover with your bodies touching: you may prefer to have your back against a wall for extra support. He keeps both feet on the ground and puts a hand on your lower back to support you while you lift one of your legs and wrap it around his waist or upper thigh. Where you place your leg depends on the difference in your heights and your suppleness. With your leg raised, he enters you and places one hand under one of your buttocks and the other under the thigh of your raised leg. This helps to pull you up onto him and keep him from slipping out.

'...pin him up against the wall, kiss

him passionately and get him

aroused quickly.'

Good for sexy, urgent sex as long as you are of approximately the same height. If you are smaller than him he will need strong legs and an ability to bend his knees for a long time.

Like Lotus, this is a beautiful, descriptive name for an elegant posture. He bent your legs over his shoulders in the Swallow, but this time his legs are wrapped around you. This feels secure and means you can wrap your arms around his legs if you choose.

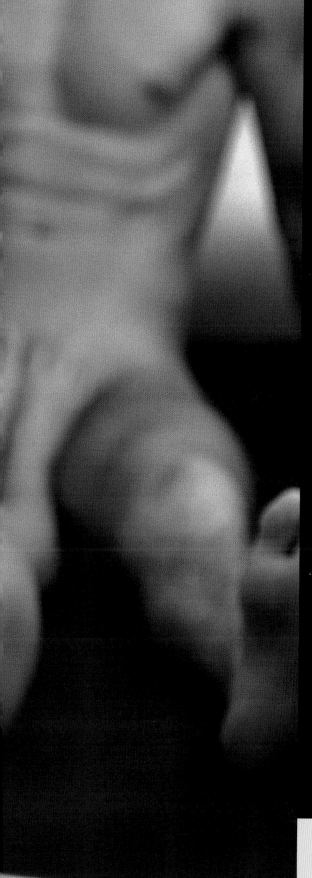

A rose in bloom

By contrast this delightful posture is perfect for when you feel like some very leisurely lovemaking.

Why it's great for women

Your lover can either play with your clitoris while penetrating you or give you oral sex before you really get into the posture. All you have to do is lie back, spread your arms wide and luxuriate in the pleasures he is giving you. You can't do much thrusting towards your lover in this posture, so all you need to do is move your hips from side to side to help vary the sensation.

What to do

Put some quilts on the floor and have your lover sit upright either with his back against the bed or the sofa. He opens his legs and lets them fall apart. You lie on your back facing him, your legs between his, and if you like you can use your feet to play with his penis – a nice bonus for him. He then raises your legs onto his shoulders and pulling your hips towards him, penetrates you. The closer you can get your buttocks in towards him, the better it is. You can stay still like this for a while, as long as he doesn't lose his erection. Then start to roll your hips together from side to side, creating sensation for both of you. Because there isn't a lot of movement, it will be easier for him to focus on playing with your clitoris and making you climax.

'...lie back, spread your arms wide and luxuriate in the pleasures he is giving you.'

Maharajah

And in return for the pleasure he gives, you can take him into this *Kama Sutra* posture that will make him feel like royalty in receipt of loving devotion while he relaxes completely.

Why it's great for women

Again this is a posture where you are in control while your lover is in a vulnerable position – his genitals exposed and his legs supported by you. This is an opportunity for you to express yourself as the embodiment of the feminine, to be a goddess and pleasure him as a woman well versed in the sexual arts.

Here is an opportunity for you to show your man what an accomplished lover he has. With his legs over your shoulders you can control the thrusts.

What to do

You sit upright with your legs falling apart and your toes pointing towards each other. Your lover sits inside your legs with his legs placed over yours and his feet behind your back. He embraces you around your shoulders while you clasp him around his waist. Before going any further, take the time to kiss him on the mouth, the face and the neck.

Then put your feet flat on the bed or floor to support yourself. He puts his arms behind him so that he can lower himself back down onto a bed piled high with cushions and pillows, so he can relax completely. When he is comfortable, he raises first one leg, then the other, over your shoulders, and you clasp him to you by holding his legs just above the knees. Now that his legs are in position, bring your legs back, bending them at the knees, your feet pointing outwards, so that you are more squatting than kneeling. Now guide your lover's penis inside you and use gentle bouncing movements to give him pleasurable sensations.

'...this is an opportunity for you to express yourself as the embodiment of the feminine.'

Drawing the bow

This sideways position is ideal for early morning sex and is excellent for when you want to wake up with your lover inside you.

Why it's great for women

Many women fantasize about waking slowly to find their lover already making love to them. There is something deeply emotionally satisfying about the idea that your lover wants you as soon as he wakes up. This posture is gentle enough for this, and can become more energetic as you become more awake and aroused. It gives you the opportunity to thrust along with your lover and as your legs are quite tight together, the sensations will be heightened.

What to do

You lie on your back facing away from your lover while he lies close behind you, in a spoons position. He lifts your upper leg and squeezes both of his legs between yours so that he is in a position to penetrate you. Once he has entered you, he places his hands on your shoulders and pulls you back towards him. You can start thrusting together at this stage of the pose, but when you feel like having some deeper penetration, bend your upper body downwards so you can grab hold of his lower legs and pull them up towards you. This is what creates the effect of a bow and arrow shape. Now you can both move your hips together, alternating strong and gentle rhythms.

This is perfect for sex in that lovely half asleep, half awake dream state. Let him know that if he wants you when you are sleeping, provided he is gentle, he should have you.

'...many women fantasize about waking slowly to find their lover already making love to them.'

The fusion of love

Side positions are always relaxing and for a woman they often provide stronger sensations than others as her legs tend to be together.

Why it's great for women

The ultimate aim of sex in the traditions of the *Kama Sutra* and Tantra is the union, or fusion, of the qualities of Shiva and Shakti – deities representing the male and female energies. As you come together to make love you are two people and when you join through penetration you become one entity in which the masculine and feminine merge to create balance. In this gentle posture you are equal, neither one being in a superior position, and it is perfect for becoming aware of your own sexual energy and how it differs from, and complements, your lover's.

What to do

You lie on your sides facing each other with your genitals touching. Pause here to feel the energy passing between your genitals. Your lover keeps his lower leg straight and lifts his other leg, wrapping it gently over your hip. Parting your legs slightly, he penetrates you, and placing your legs back together again, firmly pulls your upper thigh towards his buttocks. When he does this he may arch his body away from you so that he can penetrate you more deeply. You may ask him to thrust into you; alternatively, you can rotate your hips together or rock them back-and-forth to increase clitoral stimulation.

'...you become aware of your own sexual energy and how it differs from, and complements, your lover's.'

Sometimes it is important to give due reverence to making love. Although he controls the movements here, it is an intimate posture that should make both of you feel worshipped and able to focus on the sensations you are experiencing.

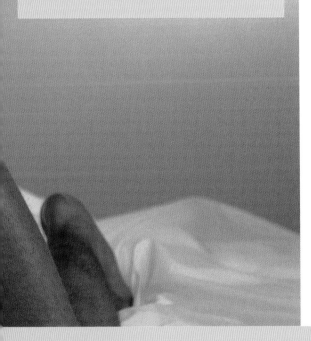

Puja

This is the first of three postures which acknowledge more clearly the spiritual aspects of sex. As such they are appropriate poses for ending sex with, which is why they also come at the end of this series of postures from the *Kama Sutra*.

Puja is a way of worship involving the daily offering of flowers or food, the lighting of incense and the utterance of a prayer before an altar of favourite gods. Sex is also a form of puja in which we offer our devotion to our lover.

Why it's great for women

In brief, this posture offers you the potential to become one with your lover as you create a closed circuit of energy between your bodies. As with the Fusion of Love, you have the opportunity to become more acquainted with your female sexual energy. Additionally, as your legs are close together in this posture you can grip your lover's penis tightly with your muscles, enhancing the experience for both of you.

What to do

You lie relaxed on your back while your lover, kneeling to face you, helps you to gently fold your knees back towards your chest. Only take them back as far as is comfortable, and if you feel any strain, release your legs a little. Now he should slide his knees to either side of your hips and place your feet against his chest so your legs are supported. Once he enters you he takes charge of all movements. He may hold your legs in place by crossing his hands over your knees as this helps him to thrust more energetically. And while your knees are held together like this you can squeeze him with your vaginal muscles.

'...puja is a way of worship involving the daily offering of flowers or food...sex is also a form of puja in which we offer our devotion to our lover.'

Another beautiful, impressive posture. Although you both need space to breathe after sex, your bodies often appreciate a little contact while they wind down from getting all that attention.

Namaste

One of the most beautiful salutations in existence, this ancient Sanskrit word means 'I bow to you', while its more spiritual meaning is, 'my soul honours your soul'. What better way to thank your lover for the experience of sharing love through your bodies?

Why it's great for women

In this posture, which is ideally a post-coital one, you are honoured by the man for the pleasure you have given him, and for your perfection as a woman, a human being and his partner on life's journey. It is a way for you to thank each other and to align yourselves with the divine through sex.

What to do

Sitting with his back straight, your lover lets his legs fall apart, bending his knees slightly. You lie on your back, your legs to either side of his thighs, your hips about level with his knees. If you wish to have penetration in this pose, your lover can enter you now, but if you are using it after sex, just keep close genital contact. Pressing your legs together and holding you by the feet, your lover gently lifts your legs up towards his face and places the soles of your feet against his mouth so that he may kiss them. He then places your feet against his nose, followed by his eyes and his forehead. Finally, he places them against the top of his head.

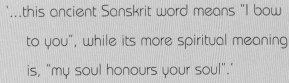

'...this ancient Sanskrit word means "I bow to you", while its more spiritual meaning is, "my soul honours your soul".'

Kissing at dawn

Strictly speaking, this is not a position but an embrace of which there are many in the *Kama Sutra* and related texts such as the *Kama Shastra*, which is book of sexual etiquette for upper class wives.

Why it's great for women

There are times when a woman wants to show her lover how much she desires him and appreciates him. This is a simple and beautiful way to show your devotion, and while some may think we are too modern for such a thing, we can learn from these ancient texts that it is precisely these types of acts which keep lovers together. Try it after showering, when your sense of smell and the feeling of warm clean skin will enhance the eroticism.

What to do

First of all, your feet must be bare. You approach your lover from the front and wind your arms around his neck, raise your face to look into his, and keeping your lips soft and slightly parted, prepare to give him an erotic kiss. You then place the soles of your feet on top of his feet and kiss him deeply. This is considered to be a very special form of salutation. If you want to take this posture further, you can raise one leg and wind it around the back of his thigh, as if your leg was a vine winding itself around him. If you wish this posture to be arousing, take extra time with the kiss, finding his tongue and biting and sucking his lower lip. However, if sex is not the priority, be sure he knows it is a token of your affection and that you have given him the promise of pleasure later.

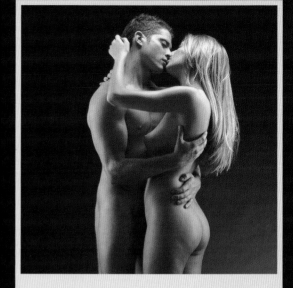

This and Namaste are reminders of what every woman knows: that there is more to lovemaking than penetration. Everybody likes to feel appreciated – or teased, if you prefer...

'...there are times when a woman wants to show her lover how much she desires him and appreciates him.'

Index

Acknowledgements

The publishers would like to thank *Agent Provocateur* for the loan of props.
www.agentprovocateur.com

Executive editor Jane McIntosh
Editor Alice Bowden

Executive art editor Geoff Fennell
Designer Simon Wilder
Photographer John Davis

Production controller Manjit Sihra